D0555796

The Upholsterer's
Step-by-Step Handbook
A Practical Reference

With thanks to Amy and Mabel.
Without their support this book
would not have been possible.

I would also like to thank all of the
upholsterers who have generously
shared their techniques and the
students who have enabled me to
define and orate them.

THE UPHOLSTERER'S STEP-BY-STEP
HANDBOOK.

Copyright © 2015 by Pavilion.
All rights reserved. Printed in China.
For information, address St. Martin's Press,
175 Fifth Avenue, New York, N.Y. 10010.

www.stmartins.com

Library of Congress Cataloging-in-Publication Data
Available Upon Request

ISBN 978-1-250-04985-8

St. Martin's Griffin books may be purchased for
educational, business, or promotional use. For
information on bulk purchases, please contact
Macmillan Corporate and Premium Sales
Department at 1-800-221-7945, extension 5442, or
write specialmarkets@macmillan.com.

First U.S. Edition: January 2015

10 9 8 7 6 5 4 3 2 1

The Upholsterer's
Step-by-Step Handbook
A Practical Reference

ALEX LAW

ST. MARTIN'S GRIFFIN
NEW YORK

Contents

Introduction

The techniques and materials of upholstery have evolved over the centuries to take on ever more complicated nuances, but in its pure form, upholstery is a set of basic rules and similar methods that can be applied to many different chairs. I am not sure how long it took for me to realize that the basic approach to upholstery didn't need to be varied from chair to chair, but that was part of my transition from bench upholsterer to upholstery tutor. By focusing on the similarities rather than the differences, it becomes clear that a few basic "cornerstone" principles can be applied to a wide variety of visual styles. Seeing through the fog of chair styles, materials and fabrics was key to my identifying the most important aspects of producing well-upholstered chairs.

Obviously it is impossible to cover all aspects of upholstery in one book so, rather than collecting many chair styles and dazzling you with the latest fabrics applied to dozens of examples, I have used my experience to break down the upholstery process and focus on the tools and techniques required to produce generic types of pad that can be adapted to a myriad of different chairs. I would be doing my mentors and peers an injustice to suggest that upholstery is easy to master, but by limiting the vast spectrum of techniques and building from the foundation of a few core techniques, you will be amazed at how many styles of upholstered chair can be successfully tackled and successfully transformed.

So whether you have inherited a masterpiece from the past, found a treat in a backstreet market on a foreign shore, conceived a new idea in the form of a chair or simply fancy applying yourself to a worthy craft, following the methods described in this book will help you to create upholstery that should stand the test of time and survive the rigors of use.

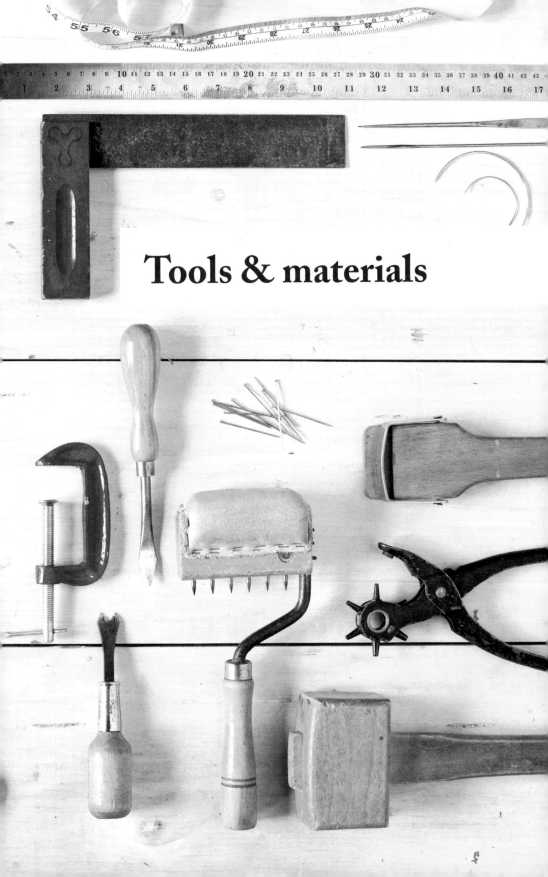

Tools & materials

CHAPTER I
Tools & materials

Hand tools

Many of the hand tools used in upholstery are specific to the craft, but there are also some general woodworking and sewing tools that have cross-over uses. You may well have some of these tools already, so there is no need to rush out and buy every tool on the market. Be aware, however, that some general tools may not be robust enough for upholstery applications. This is a brief overview of what you will need and the pros and cons of different types. It is a personal selection and not exhaustive: every upholsterer has his or her own preferences but, if you're new to upholstery, the list below is a good starting point.

Tools for ripping down

Ripping down—otherwise known as stripping out—the old upholstery is generally the starting point for most projects. It can mean anything from simply removing the existing covering carefully so as to not disturb the stuffing layers underneath, right through to removing all of the upholstery, including any broken tacks or staples, in order to repair or renovate the frame.

Mallets

The principal use of a mallet is to deliver a short, sharp burst of force to the tool you are using. It will often help to knock out tacks and staples in fewer attempts than simply digging or poking at the fixing with a chisel or tack lifter. Mallets are also useful when carefully tapping frame joints apart and occasionally "persuading" things to fit. It can take a few hours to remove the existing upholstery from even small chairs and possibly even days for much larger pieces of furniture, so you need to feel comfortable wielding the mallet you have chosen. Your choice of mallet depends more on the material you are tapping than on the shape of the mallet head: for materials that are likely to shatter on impact or where you might damage the fabric—for example, plastic wood-effect components—a rubber-headed mallet is best. However, your choice will also be determined by the space in which you have to work (smaller mallets for smaller spaces) and the amount of force you need to apply (heavier mallets where more force is required).

Most people who have done any kind of woodworking in the past will have a wooden **carpenter's mallet**. These tend to be made of beech and the heads are square in appearance. They come in different weights and sizes and I recommend one with a head size of around 6 x 4" (15 x 10 cm); it is lightweight and its relatively small size makes it easy to swing it around inside the confines of a chair frame.

Mallets

1 Carpenter's mallet

2 Wooden round-headed mallet

3 Rubber round-headed mallet

Round-headed mallets are made in a variety of materials and can range from lightweight camping mallets to large-headed mallets used for tamping pre-cast concrete slabs. **Wooden round-headed mallets** are similar to the square carpenter's mallet but, as there is less wood in the head, they are slightly lighter than a carpenter's mallet of a similar size and wood type. They are useful for general applications, but their compact nature and lighter weight require a firmer strike to deliver the same impact as a square mallet.

Rubber round-headed mallets are made from a dense, vulcanized rubber and can be used for most processes. The rubber dulls the sound when hitting another tool, so they are quieter to work with; I often use one when a colleague is on the phone to a customer or when I am simply listening to a good play on the radio. They are also handy when tapping rails or non-metal components, as they are less likely to bruise or shatter the thing that you are tapping.

Nylon-headed and **hickory barrel-shaped mallets** are heavier than beech or rubber round-headed mallets and are only really useful when a good clout is required, so they are the least frequently used types of mallet. It can be very useful to have one in your tool kit—if you can afford the space to have a mallet that you use only a few times a year.

Ripping chisels

The main aim of a ripping chisel is to lift tacks out of a wooden rail cleanly and efficiently, without biting into the rail. Upholsterer's ripping chisels are very different from carpenter's chisels, in that the bevel or sharp end is not honed to anywhere near as sharp a point. A carpenter's chisel will blunt extremely quickly and could fracture, allowing small fragments to fly off, which could be very dangerous if they flew into your

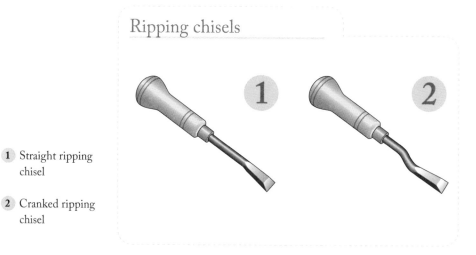

Ripping chisels

1 Straight ripping chisel

2 Cranked ripping chisel

eye. (I can't imagine that you'd get a warm reception from the carpenter either if you returned a battered chisel that had taken hours to sharpen and hone.)

There are two types: the **straight ripping chisel** and the **cranked ripping chisel**. Both types are usually made from drop-forged steel, which makes the steel harder, and are typically set into a wooden handle. The handle shapes tend to vary from manufacturer to manufacturer. I advise newcomers to upholstery to buy a straight ripping chisel with a mushroom-shaped handle. The straight metal shaft is direct and will allow you to work in tighter spaces, while the mushroom-shaped handle will help protect your hand. The cranked ripper is better suited to lighter work where greater accuracy is required.

It is also worth mentioning the **split-headed tack lifter**. This is a kind of ripping chisel with a flattened, curved end to the metal shaft and an elongated, pear-shaped handle. This tool is excellent for removing tacks in a more controlled way, as the tack is cupped by the split in the tool head and cleanly lifts away from the wood. It is also handy when you have to carefully remove a piece of fabric that you intend to replace later in the project.

Staple removers

Staple removers also come in a variety of styles. The three most commonly used in upholstery are spade-type, Berry and Osborne staple removers. They are easy to identify, as they are so different in both appearance and use. None that I have ever encountered is a surefire way of removing the whole staple every time and invariably the spikes of metal left require extracting or tapping in. For more on how to remove staples, turn to page 87.

The **spade-type staple remover** is generally found in every upholstery workshop. The handle and metal shaft make it similar in appearance to the tack lifter but its head is, as the name suggests, spade like. This makes it easy to slip it under a staple and then lift the staple by applying downward force to the handle. You can also rotate the tool a little if it helps to get some extra lift. The flat nature of this tool means that the wood is less likely to be bruised by it than by the other two main types of staple remover.

The **Berry staple remover** is a trademarked tool with a distinctive wide head and short body. Its hardened head (which, to my mind, resembles the top half of the Batman logo!) can be used to lift and extract the staple. The shaft of the tool is short and the generous metal collar binds the tang into its stubby handle, which fits neatly into the user's hand. By poking one of the two prongs under one end of a staple, it's fairly easy to

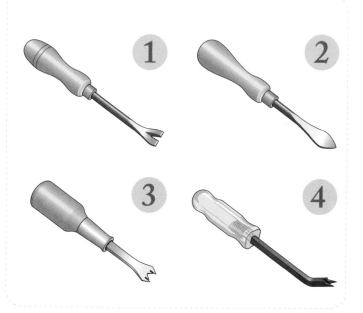

1 Split-headed tack lifter

2 Spade-type staple remover

3 Berry staple remover

4 Osborne staple lifter

get a good purchase and with a twist of the wrist one prong of the staple will lift. It is then possible to wrap the staple around the head of the staple remover and pull the staple out. The poke-and-twist motion of this tool lends itself to the rapid removal of staples and it is most commonly used when speed is of the essence. It can take a while to get used to and during long periods of stripping out you may experience a little discomfort until you have acquired the correct technique.

The **Osborne staple lifter** is another trademarked tool, the shape of which is exclusive to the manufacturer. This, too, is a steel tool with hardened prongs, but the shaft is similar in shape to the shaft of the spade-type lifter. It has a clear resin handle that is designed to not slip in the hand and is hard enough to take a lifetime of tapping. The forked head is designed to slip under the whole staple like a spade-type staple lifter or to hook around one prong of the staple like the Berry staple remover. As the tool has a narrow head, however, it is not as effective when used with a twisting motion; instead, it relies on pushing with the hand or tapping with a mallet. With a clean tap this lifter can get the odd staple out in one go, but I tend to use it on difficult-to-reach staples and then use another tool to extract the rest of the staple.

Pincers and pliers

1 Carpenter's pincers

2 Long-nosed pliers

3 Side cutters

4 General pliers

Pincers, pliers and side cutters

These key tools are used to remove stubborn fragments of tacks and staples that are stuck fast in the wooden frame, often silently waiting to catch you or someone else out later on. Ensuring that your ripping down is done so that no fragments remain is an important lesson to learn. A good pair of **general pliers** will be a useful addition to your tool kit.

We use the term **carpenter's pincers**, but in truth most carpenter's pincers are too sharp when new. Using a fine metal file to blunt or dull the jaws a little will help them to grip a staple rather than bite through it. Obviously, by the time they have been blunted slightly, they will not exactly bite through wire—instead, they sort of chew it—so if you do need them for wire cutting, don't file your only pair.

Long-nosed pliers come into their own when attempting to extract hard-to-reach staples.

Where pincers are too large or approach the staple from the wrong angle, **side cutters** are useful. These are often sharpened right down to the point. Curiously, my preferred side cutters are the ones where I haven't dulled the edge with a fine file. It appears that, due to the shape of the handles and the way the tool head is worked from side to side, the force that you can apply with side cutters isn't enough to instantly cut through the wire if the edge has been dulled.

Specialist upholstery tools

The tools listed below are specialist tools that you will need to use throughout the upholstery process. As with general tools, you don't need to go out and buy every single one; try them out and see what works for you.

Upholsterer's hammers

These come in a variety of styles and have their own intrinsic uses. The most common style of hammer used today in traditional upholstery is the **magnetic tacking hammer**. The magnetic end is either split or more slender than the hitting end and is used as if it were an extra hand. As your skill with it develops, you can use the magnet to pick up tacks and then, with a well-aimed swing, put a tack into the wood where it's required while maintaining tension on the material being fitted. Do not knock the tack home with the magnetic end, as this will de-magnetize the head of the hammer over prolonged use. Once you have placed the tack where you want it, flip the hammer head around with a simple flick of the wrist and use the more robust end to hit the tack home.

The most common style with two similar-shaped heads is cast in bronze, with steel tips fused to the bronze. This is my favored type of hammer for upholstery and I have two weights of head—one weighing approximately

Hammers

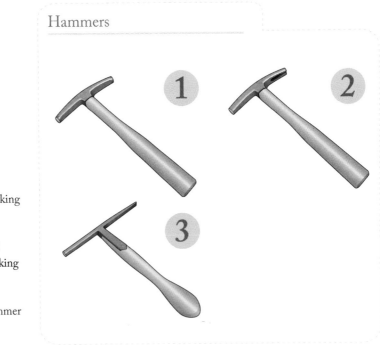

1. Magnetic tacking hammer

2. Split-headed magnetic tacking hammer

3. Cabriole hammer

7 oz (200 grams), which is my workhorse hammer, and a heavier one weighing 9 oz (255 grams), which I use mainly for hitting larger nails rather than tacks or broken staples as it delivers a heavier blow with the same amount of swing.

Magnetic hammers were not always available and there are a few upholsterers around working today who remember their introduction well; rather like the staple gun, their introduction was apparently met with some skepticism. The **original tacking hammer** had a tacking head, as we use today, but the opposite head was more of a chisel-point shape and was often forked. The forked end was used during ripping down in a similar way to the tack lifter or ripping chisel.

Prior to the introduction of magnetic hammers, upholsterers would push the tack into place with one hand and then strike the tack with the hammer; because the tacks were frequently held in the mouth of the upholsterer, the term "spitting tacks" was widely used. Even now, the careful placement of tacks rather than the slightly random positioning of the tack with the magnetic end is essential when tacking into a delicate rail or awkward-to-reach place.

An elegantly slim version of the upholsterer's hammer is known as a **cabriole hammer.** Uniquely balanced and capable of fitting into the tightest of spaces, they really are a specialist tool. They can be difficult to source nowadays, but they are well worth having in your tool kit if you get the chance.

I should also mention here the **pneumatic staple gun** which has, for at least 40 years, largely replaced the tack-and-hammer approach to upholstery, enabling upholsterers to speed up processes no end. For more information on staple guns, turn to page 32.

Upholstery shears and scissors

Is it possible to own too many pairs? Probably, but that is more likely to be due to hanging on to old pairs that are long past their best but are emotionally hard to let go of, rather than to rushing out and buying every style on the market.

Scissors or larger shears are such a personal preference that it's hard to know where to start so I will begin with 8" (20 cm) or 10" (25 cm) **blunt-nosed shears**. Designed not to snag or catch fabric other than the piece you are cutting when working in awkward areas, these shears are an essential tool for any upholsterer's tool kit. The top blade has a flattened point (hence the name, blunt-nosed), while the bottom set is curved, as in most conventional shears. It is important to use the shears the right way up when cutting along a flat surface, so that the lay of the cloth is not distorted while you are cutting. As well as not catching other panels

Scissors and shears

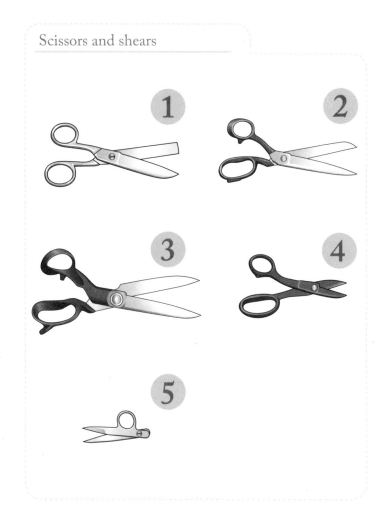

1 Blunt-nosed
shears

2 10" (25 cm)
tailor's shears

3 12" (30 cm)
tailor's shears

4 Short-bladed
scissors

5 Thread snips

of cloth in areas where two or more panels converge, the blunt nose helps prevent knocking the two blades out of alignment if you accidentally drop them onto a hard floor. (This should, of course, never happen to a master of the craft—but if you are a mere human, it may well do and it's best to be prepared.)

Cast **bent-handled** or **tailor's shears** are the classic shape of shears and they come in a variety of sizes. Shears with 10" (25 cm) blades are probably the most commonly used. Different manufacturers have their own designs and features and it's really down to individual preference as to which ones to choose. After trying various styles over the years, I currently prefer a pair that has a slightly serrated edge on one blade. These serrations help to stabilize the cloth that is being cut and help me to hold a straight line when cutting along the warp or the weft of the cloth. The serrations also bite through any tough areas of weave without your hand really experiencing any change in pressure.

A heavier pair of 12" (30 cm) bent-handled shears is also very useful. The extra weight is negated by resting the bottom blade on the cutting-table surface—and in fact, the weight makes it easier to cut through the cloth, so with prolonged use it's actually easier on your hand muscles. The extra length of the blade reduces the number of cutting operations, too. This might seem like a minor consideration at first, but after a long day's cutting out, your hand will be grateful for anything that reduces the repetition. So don't be put off by how massive they appear—you honestly don't need to have hands like paddles to use them effectively.

Short-bladed scissors with disproportionately long handles are great for cutting through multiple layers of fabrics or really tough areas. With the fulcrum so far forward, they are probably the best evolution in upholstery scissors that I have seen in my time in the craft. With a pair of these, the days of clamping two hands around the shears and turning red in the face through the exertion of chopping off an unwanted tail of piping or cutting a well-tied hitch knot from a broken spring are long gone.

A small pair of **thread snips** is a useful and inexpensive addition to your tool kit. Exclusively used for chopping sewing machine threads, they fit neatly into the storage drawer of most sewing machines and are lightweight and much easier to wield than larger shears while machining panels together or unpicking or adjusting existing machining.

Webbing stretchers

Webbing provides the foundation for everything else—springs, stuffing, upholstery fabric—in a seat base. Natural-fiber webbing (jute or linen) needs to be tensioned when it is fitted onto the frame. You attach the webbing to one side of the frame, fit it into a special upholstery tool known as a webbing stretcher (or strainer) and then run it across to the other side of the frame. The stretcher keeps the webbing under tension so that, when you fix it to the second side, it is taut enough to provide a strong, weight-bearing foundation. Using this tool means that you can stretch the webbing tighter than you could using your hands alone. Webbing stretchers are not required for rubber or elasticated webbing; with these, you need to develop a feel for the amount of stretch and tension the webbing is under by stretching it across the frame by hand.

There are small differences in webbing stretchers from one country to another, as the standard width of the webbing being used dictates the size of the webbing stretcher's mouth. In the United States and France, for example, webbing tends to be 2½" (6 cm) wide, whereas in the United Kingdom it is 2" (5 cm) wide.

For more information on attaching webbing, turn to page 107.

There are three main types of webbing stretcher. The first type is a **slot-and-peg stretcher**, in which the webbing is slotted through and held tight in place by a wooden dowel, which you have to remove once the webbing has been stretched into position.

Less common is the **latch stretcher**, in which the mechanism holding the webbing in place is a quick-release metal latch. It will save what may feel like a tiny amount of time on just one web, but if you are applying dozens, those few moments per web can add up to a substantial time saving.

The third type of webbing stretcher is used widely throughout North America. It is called a **goose-** or **swan-neck stretcher** and uses spikes to simply grip the webbing while levering the tool against the frame. Unfortunately, modern jute or black-and-white webbings do not have the same durability as the webbings available just a few years ago and they tend to shred under tensioning around the spikes, which is a mixed blessing. On one hand, this means that it is almost impossible to break a frame joint due to over-tensioning the webbing, but it also wastes a small amount of webbing every time. Where this tool comes into its own is when applying webbing to a curved frame: in addition to levering the handle up and down to tension the webbing, you can also twist or rotate the handle from side to side to prevent the tool from slipping around the

Webbing stretchers

1 Slot-and-peg stretcher

2 Latch stretcher

3 Goose- or swan-neck stretcher

4 Leather stretcher or hide dog

curve as you apply pressure. I have padded the head end of mine with some 1" (2.5-cm) thick foam and covered that with leather, which both protects any show wood and aids the stretcher in gripping the rail.

Although they are not really web stretchers per se, I should also mention leather stretchers or **hide dogs**. These pincer-like tools were (as the name suggests) designed for tensioning leather panels at a time when hide was much tougher than the supple leather we know and enjoy using today. Hide dogs are not a perfect tool for web stretching, but they are excellent for re-tensioning existing webbing when there is not enough turning or fold in the web end to use any of the three previously mentioned stretchers. They only work well if the webbing is robust enough to cope with the force applied. You must remove the tacks or staples carefully, or you will simply tear off the end of the web where it has been weakened by the previous fixings. Hide dogs are not an essential starter tool, but anyone serious about upholstering professionally should own a pair.

Upholsterer's needles

The needles used in upholstery are numerous, and you will need a range of different shapes and sizes.

The largest needles that are used almost daily in traditional upholstery and are useful for buttoning are **double-pointed needles**. They have two pointed ends and speed up a great variety of processes. Needles that are 8–12" (20–30 cm) long tend to be made from 13-gauge wire, while 16" (40-cm) needles are made from a slightly thicker 12-gauge wire. The ends or points of these needles are either round in cross section or bayonet. A basic rule of thumb is that the round-point needles are best for use on woven cloths, while bayonet points are better for slicing their way through leather and batting. Long, single-point buttoning needles are still used in upholstery, but their use is fairly limited.

Springing needles are usually 5" (12.5 cm) long. Designed (as the name suggests) to cut through the webbing when attaching springs, they are curved, with the eye at the blunt end and the sharp end flattened out into a blade point. They are made from much thicker wire than buttoning needles and I find that a springing needle is likely to cut too many fibers of the webbing as it is pushed through. Webbing quality fluctuates at best and generally isn't as tightly woven as it once was, so I prefer to avoid compromising the integrity of the weave by using another slimmer needle. Instead of a springing needle, I tend to use a 5" or 6" (12.5-cm or 15-cm) **curved needle** with a bayonet point and a gauge of around 13. These are the largest of the curved needles frequently used in upholstery. Single-point curved needles are available in sizes ranging from 6" (15 cm) down to 2" (5 cm) and are available in all manner of gauges at each length.

Needles, skewers, and pins

1 Bayonet double-pointed needle (top); round double-pointed needle (bottom)

2 Springing needle

3 Slipping needles

4 Regulator

5 Wooden pleating tool

6 Upholstery skewers

7 Upholstery pins

Not shown to scale.

Slipping needles are at the opposite end of the spectrum in size and are used for slipstitching or castle stitching (see page 214) and doing blanket stitches with finer threads. Although upholsterers will develop their own preferences for slipstitching needles, it is unusual to see conventional straight needles used for any hand-sewing process in upholstery.

One of the most distinctive needles used in upholstery doesn't really ever have a thread placed through its eye and is called a **regulator**. Its flattened eye end is held in the hand and the point is used in a variety of operations, from moving stuffing around during edge stitching to manipulating fabric. It is not uncommon to hear it described as the upholsterer's best and most versatile tool. Regulators are made from steel wire and are available in various sizes, from a mini 6" (15 cm) to a robust 12" (30 cm) 6-gauge type. They have also evolved to have solid flattened metal heads or even plastic handles reminiscent of an ice pick.

One drawback with the traditional steel regulator is that, like all untreated metal, it can rust. Discovering rust being transferred onto your fabric while using the regulator to manipulate the cover into something like a pleat is distressing, to say the least. This can be avoided by using a **wooden pleating tool** (also known as a wooden dolly). Made from hardwood, the pleater has to be thick enough not to snap, and smooth enough to glide through its operations without scoring the fabric. I have a couple of these that I use regularly. More recently I have been using an acrylic version based on a bone tool used by leatherworkers that appears to fit the bill very well indeed.

Skewers and pins
Upholstery skewers play an important role in holding traditional upholstery materials together during stitching processes and can be used for many purposes, including marking out measured distances, lightly manipulating stuffings and dabbing glue into hard-to-reach places. They come in two basic forms. The standard type is made from a single length of wire and bent to form a loop at one end; European skewers have a blob of acrylic at the non-pointed end. Both styles are useful. I find the European type a little flimsy for more robust applications, but the acrylic end is far less likely to snag or catch on open or loosely woven textiles. I'm confident that you will find both types of skewers worth owning. They come in lengths ranging from 3–5" (7.5–12.5 cm).

Steel **upholstery pins** are like skewers, in that they are coated to prevent them from rusting as they are frequently used when positioning fabrics. Generally they are much more robust and perhaps a little longer than pins used in soft furnishings or dressmaking. Occasionally, glass-headed pins are used by upholsterers, but on the whole they tend to be a little flimsy for everything except pinning pieces of fabric together before sewing on a machine.

Tools for marking out cloth

Being able to clearly mark out any piece of cloth is essential and there are a few standard pieces of equipment that will help to ensure accuracy. Some will be familiar to anyone who has previously had an interest in textile crafts and you may own a few of them already.

Tape measures and yardsticks

Flexible fabric **tape measures** are useful when measuring panels on a chair, as you can easily stretch them around both the outside and inside of curves to obtain accurate measurements.

Rigid rulers or **yardsticks** are important for marking out for a number of reasons. Unlike tape measures, yardsticks don't contract or fold inadvertently, so they can be moved around over the cloth easily, they have an edge that can be chalked along without slipping, and they can help to flatten a piece of cloth during marking and prevent the cloth from "creeping" while being chalked. It is advisable to have at least one that is longer than the width of a roll of fabric, the most common width for upholstery fabric being 54" (140 cm). Yardsticks are available in wood or steel alloy in various lengths, and a good combination to have is one or two wooden 3-feet (1-meter) rulers and a single 60" (150-cm) alloy rule, 2" (5 cm) wide. I like using steel rules, but being steel they can and do rust a little so it is best to avoid using one to mark out fabric prior to cutting.

Marking squares

A **marking square** is a useful addition to any cutting table. They come in three basic shapes: the most common triangular type, L-shaped and T-shaped. Each has its benefits. A clear acrylic triangular square is great for accurate close-up marking of patterned fabrics where pattern matching the details is vital. Large L-shaped builders' marking squares are made from steel, but they are coated with paint for outdoor use so will not transfer rust to the cloth for many years. They are relatively heavy, so not only do they denote a right angle, but they also weigh the fabric down, which is very helpful when laying out a cloth that has a pile or has a wobbly warp or weft. T-shaped squares hook onto the outside of the cutting table and are the least commonly used of the three. So long as the cloth's selvedge is parallel to the cutting table edge, a T-square is most useful when checking and marking where a pattern is positioned as it repeats up the roll, prior to marking a line across the roll width. A useful addition is a T-square where the head is at a 45-degree angle to the shaft instead of 90 degrees; this makes it a very useful tool for marking out piping on the bias.

Dividers are very useful for marking out spacing evenly and **a protractor** will help with any angles not found on a standard marking square.

Measuring and marking tools

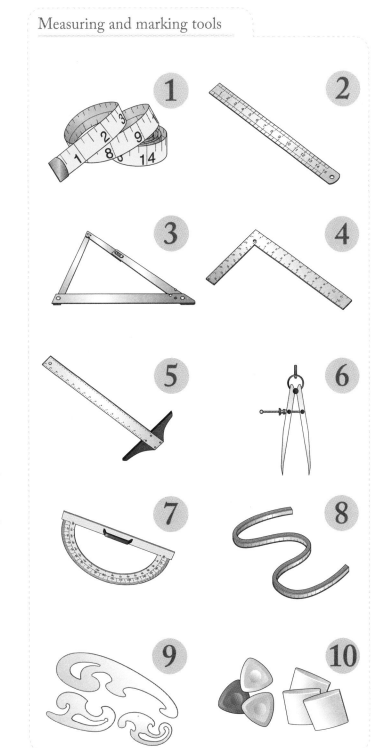

1 Flexible fabric tape measure

2 Steel yardstick

3 Triangular marking square

4 L-shaped marking square

5 T-square

6 Dividers

7 Protractor

8 Flexi curve

9 French curves

10 Tailor's chalk

Tools for marking out curves

Marking out curves can be one of the hardest operations when you are working on your own, and I am very much of the school of thinking that to mark a curve quickly and accurately, it's best to have two upholsterers there—one to bend an acrylic straight edge to form the curve and a second one to chalk the line. Tools that can help in marking curves include a large compass, a flexi curve and a French curve.

When using a large **compass** it is important to avoid snagging the weave of the cloth with the needle end, otherwise re-dressing the cloth's weave into place won't be possible after marking out. If you are using a large compass that takes board chalk, it's important to sharpen one edge so that you don't end up drawing too thick a line, as it doesn't give a precise enough line to cut along.

Flexi curves and **French curves** are used in pattern-making. When you need to mark out an asymmetric shape or if you're trying to copy a shape, a flexi curve can be bent to the shape required and will hold its shape once removed so that you can draw along the edge and create your pattern. A French curve is a rigid tool formed into a series of arcs; you select the one that matches the curve you want and draw around it on your pattern paper or fabric.

When a set of complicated interlinking curves or a large span is required, don't waste huge amounts of time and potentially waste expensive fabric, but instead, mark and cut a template from cardboard or muslin (calico).

Tailor's chalk

Tailor's chalk is made in either square or triangular pieces and in pencil form, although I personally think it's better to avoid the pencil form for larger projects. With square and triangular pieces, the edges are honed or sharpened slightly to keep the line thinner and should be sharpened during marking out to keep the width of the line consistent. Unlike board chalk, which is very powdery, tailor's chalk is waxed, which means that it stays in the cloth for longer. It comes in different colors; ideally, choose one that is similar to the base cloth, so that it blends in as much as possible, as it isn't always possible to blow off unwanted chalk marks thoroughly.

Marking wax

Shaped like tailor's chalk, this pure wax is used for marking out on leather, where the chalk marks would simply slide off the surface.

1 Sash cramp

2 G-clamp

3 Speed cramp

4 Ratchet strap

Tools for basic wooden frame repairs

If your frame requires major repairs, it's generally best to take it to a furniture restorer. However, minor repairs such as re-gluing corner blocks are relatively easy and you will need a small selection of basic tools for this purpose.

For more information on basic frame repairs, turn to page 89.

Clamps and cramps

You will need a selection of cramps and clamps to hold pieces while glue is drying or to fix them in position on the workbench while you're working on them. Before investing too heavily, think about how frequently you will use them and what clamps or cramps suit the kinds of repairs that you will encounter most often.

Sash cramps are designed to pull things together over a distance, for example, when gluing the side rails of a chair to the front rail. There is no need to spend a fortune on oversized top-of-the-range types. Initially, I would opt for a couple of sash cramps that are around 3 feet (1 meter) or so in length and build your collection from there. It is very easy to

Files and planes

1 Carpenter's chisel

2 Woodworker's file

3 Block plane

4 Smoothing plane

5 Rasp

6 Surform shaver

7 Surform plane

adjust the tension on sash cramps, so there is less risk of overtightening the frame and snapping the joint. It is best to store sash cramps flat: if you lean them upright against a wall or in a cupboard, they often fall over.

G-clamps do not have a wide throat, so they are used for clamping smaller blocks and pieces with greater precision. Because they have a screw-thread tightening mechanism, you can tighten them to apply a considerable amount of force. They can, however, be overtightened and cheaper castings are more likely to twist than quality examples.

Speed cramps do all the lighter jobs that G-clamps can do, for example, holding a block in place while you are screwing it securely. The advantage is that they can be worked with one hand and applied and released quickly. Their limitations are based on the strength of the user, as there is no gearing mechanism. There is probably more variation in quality with speed cramps than with the other types of cramp or clamp.

Increasingly, **ratchet straps** are being produced specifically for woodworking, which is a far cry from the heavy lugage straps that I first saw being used in a cabinet-making workshop. Similar to roof rack straps for a car but with an added ratchet mechanism that means they can tighten up and distribute the pressure evenly along their length, these straps are becoming a workshop essential when re-gluing anything with curved rails.

A makeshift and inexpensive alternative is a **bicycle inner tube**. Remove it and cut off the valve, soak in hot water for a few minutes, dry the rubber, then wrap around the item being clamped. As the rubber cools, it will contract, applying pressure where needed. This is particularly useful if you're trying to re-attach awkwardly shaped objects that a conventional clamp would slip off.

So if your budget will allow, then I would choose to have two sash cramps, at least one 6" (15-cm) and one 9" (23-cm) G-clamp, a couple of standard speed cramps and a ratchet strap.

Chisels

Carpenter's chisels are very useful for cleaning up wood around old joints. As with ripping chisels, dulling the sharp blades of carpenter's chisels by scraping off old glue is not the done thing, so you could consider buying some already used chisels for this, as they should be extremely cheap. However, attempting to chisel wood away with a blunt chisel will lead to a crude job and probably an injury—just like kitchen knives, it's the blunt ones that tend to slip and cut you. Sets of carpenter's chisels don't have to be expensive, but spending a little extra on good steel is rarely regretted, as you will need only minimum pressure to remove thin slithers of wood and the strong cutting edge will bite into most hardwoods cleanly. If your budget will not stretch to a full set of five or six carpenter's chisels, then a ½" (12-mm) and 1" (2.5-cm) blade should suffice.

Files, rasps and surforms

Files, rasps and surforms are all used for removing wood. A **woodworker's file** will clog up very quickly, and should be reserved for old, dry, dense hardwoods where perhaps a beveled tacking edge is in need of tidying prior to re-upholstering and a rasp might be too coarse. Its main use is on metal, when you've cut through an old fixing with a hack saw and need to tidy up and smooth the cut end. You can clean a file's teeth using a dry nailbrush.

Used for softening and chamfering the edges of new hardwood rails and board materials, a **block plane** can be a very useful addition to your kit. The same applies to a **smoothing plane** (the classic shape of carpenter's plane); however, the disadvantage is that you need to use both hands to apply firm pressure and, because of its size, it is more difficult to access some rails. Whenever possible on an old frame, use a file rather than a block or smoothing plane, as there will always be a risk of a broken tack shaft scoring and blunting the plane blade.

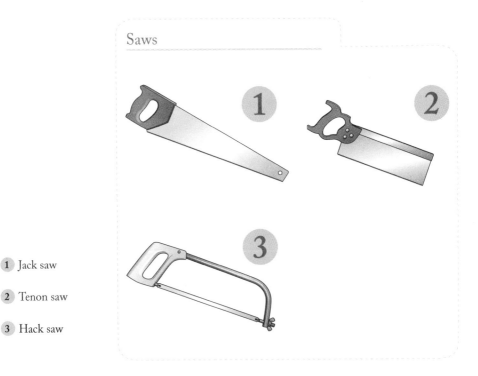

Saws

1 Jack saw

2 Tenon saw

3 Hack saw

The **rasp** is the most commonly used file-like tool for removing sharp edges on new hardwood frames and for rounding board materials such as chipboards used in headboards. It is not as fine-toothed as a file, which is really designed for use on metal. It is possible to be too enthusiastic and remove too much when rasping chipboards and other materials that crumble on the edges, so some care is required.

A **surform** is similar to a rasp and is great for quickly removing material and shaping the edges of particle board materials rather than solid hardwoods.

Saws
Saws come in a vast array of sizes and styles, with teeth set to cut in different ways, but there are three saws that should be part of every upholsterer's kit.

The first is a standard carpenter's **jack saw** which, when kept sharp, will cut most board materials and timber that you will encounter. The saws themselves are not all universal, but some are; in these, the teeth will be ground and honed to cope with cutting both along and across the wood grain. To help prevent the blade from wobbling around while you are cutting, grasp the handle and point your forefinger along it toward the narrow end of the saw.

For finer cuts, the conventional choice used to be a **tenon saw**, as the teeth are set very close together and the blade is narrower. It has a brass bar along the top of the blade, which keeps it stable while you are cutting. Designed principally to cut across the grain of the wood, this type of saw is synonymous with craftsmanship and most larger workshops probably have several hanging up and dotted around. For this type of cutting I have always preferred saws that have the teeth set so that the cutting occurs as the saw is drawn toward the body, rather than a conventional set that cuts when the saw is pushed away, giving you more control. Originally from Japan, this style of saw—called a **pull saw**—is simple and elegant to use. They are becoming increasingly common, with many companies adding to their ranges by producing a few sizes that make fantastic alternatives to tenon saws.

The third type of important saw is a **hack saw**. Used for cutting through metal, this style of saw is frequently used to release metal fittings where casters have broken or screw heads have rusted and crumbled away and cannot be removed. Hack saw bodies vary widely; it's best to avoid smaller types, because the larger ones hold deeper-set blades, which are stronger. The handle need not be expensive as it's the blades that are worth the investment.

Air and power tools

The introduction of compressed air tools was a significant development in twentieth-century tool manufacture. The great advantage of compressed air tools is that, because the air is compressed in one central location, the tools themselves don't need to contain electric motors, so there are fewer components to malfunction and the actual tool heads themselves are much lighter. Cordless tools are another recent development. As the tools have become better and more reliable, battery technology, too, has improved. Consequently, upholstery tacking and stapling processes have become quicker and less physically demanding. As an upholsterer who began my career in 1989, I find it hard to comprehend how upholsterers made furniture on a commercially viable time frame using only hand tools.

Drills

I really do find the array of drills baffling. Whether you go for a corded or cordless type, attempting to select the right one feels like something of a lottery. What's certain is that when drilling hardwood and metal you need a powerful drill yet one that is not too bulky or heavy. It is possible to spend the same amount on a drill as on an average silent compressor and staple gun kit, so equating cost to benefit is not impossible in anything other than very general terms. For professional daily use, invest as much as you can reasonably afford in a simple drill that is around 18 volts or equivalent. You will need good-quality drill bit and screw fittings, too, as cheaper ones break very easily. Remember: buy well, buy once; buy cheaply, buy often.

Staple guns and compressors

Very few upholsterers would argue against the pneumatic air staple gun being the single most important tool in the industry today. I have met some talented upholsterers who simply have not placed a tack or wielded a magnetic hammer for years. The two types of staple you will encounter are the 71 and the 53 series (see page 41). You will need a different staple gun for each. When starting out, it is probably only worth investing in a 71 series gun, as the 53 series is more specialist.

When it comes to choosing a staple gun, size, weight, and casting quality are all factors to consider. With the rise of second-hand tool trading on the Internet, it is now possible to get a good-quality second-hand gun and have it serviced, and I would advise doing this rather than buying a budget new gun. I'm reluctant to recommend one type of gun over others, as this may not be the type best suited to you, so do your homework and

1 Staple guns

2 Long nosed staple gun

3 Electric bread knife

4 Foam cutter

5 Fabric cutter with circular blade

6 Fabric cutter with vertical blade

try out a few. A good upholstery supplier will be able to supply a key tool like this on approval.

Of course, you also need to consider how the gun is powered. The gun itself is very basic in design, but choosing a suitable air compressor and the accessories can be daunting. The size of the compressor is often the first hurdle. Then consider how portable and how quiet it needs to be.

Small, non-silent compressors are the most cost-effective solution, but they can be antisocial, especially if you are starting out from home or sharing a workspace with other people. So-called "silent" compressors aren't completely silent, but they are about as quiet as an average kitchen fridge. There are, of course, cost implications: a standard oil-filled silent compressor is likely to be around 2.5 times more expensive than a standard oil-filled electric motor compressor. Oil-less compressors have recently become much more affordable, bringing them within the budget of serious amateurs and semi-professionals.

A 4–6½-gallon (15–24-liter) tank and one motor would serve one gun for light use. For day-long use with perhaps two tools running off one compressor, I would suggest considering a larger tank. In a larger workshop where a permanent compressor is needed, running perhaps four or five guns, you could consider installing a central compressor unit with at least a 13-gallon (50-liter) tank that would deliver air to all the airlines at a constant pressure, through plumbed-in metal air pipes connected to flexible air hoses at each workstation.

Good-quality high-pressure air couplings are essential for building a system that doesn't leak air. The push fittings tend to come in two types: the branded PCL connection system and the more generic quick-release connectors. PCL connectors are very well made, but are a little longer fitting so I personally stick to the stubby quick-release type and use hose clamps for all hose connections. Two- or three-ply rubber air hosepipe is fantastically resilient and less likely to be punctured, but due to its cost and weight the clear reinforced plastic pipe has become the most commonly used type in upholstery workshops.

Electric cutting tools

Electric cutting tools take a lot of the hard work out of cutting both fabric and foam, but think about how much you're likely to use them before you invest in really expensive, specialist pieces of kit.

Bread knife

The electric bread knife has been a budget foam-cutting tool since its invention and still has a place in most workshops as a fast, easy-to-use and (best of all) very cheap way of trimming and cutting most single-density foam up to around 4" (10 cm) thick. There is no point in pretending that you could run a professional foam conversion business with one of these, but if you need an open-ended hand-held cutter for occasional use, then it's fine. I try to pick up second-hand ones from flea markets, because the older ones can cut to the tip whereas the more recent models have safety tips that prevent you from cutting along the entire length of the blade. And if the cost is very low and the motor dies within six months, it's not a financial disaster.

Foam cutter

Bosch manufactures the most common hand-held tool designed specifically for foam cutting. You can buy a head unit and base trundle separately and then choose the blade length best suited to your needs. The complete blade is made from two thin blades placed together—similar to bread and meat knives, but with the set of the much finer teeth inverted. This action gives a fairly clean fine cut and the blade base with its mini castors allows you to cut vertically through laminated layers of foam and reconstituted foam. When the base is detached, the cutter can be used to cut beveled edges or shapes following a former or pattern. The quality motor can cope with extended periods of use. The initial outlay is around the same as a good staple gun and small, silent compressor kit, but for the professional upholsterer it's a must-have tool.

Electric fabric cutters

Electric fabric cutters are useful if you're the poor soul who has to spend days at a time at the cutting table. These tools are absolutely essential in larger manufacturing environments, but are also useful in smaller shops for cutting out around templates or cutting multiple layers. If you're new to upholstery, or only planning to do it as a hobby from time to time, then electric fabric cutters are not a necessity.

The cutters can be crudely classed into two types: those that have a vertical blade or those with circular cutting blades. Each blade type has a variety of styles and sizes. Vertical blades are very heavy and have to be table mounted; however, they can cut through many layers and they do make very accurate foam cutters. Cutters with circular blades are principally used for cutting just one or two layers of cloth and are not suited to cutting foam.

Industrial sewing machines and sundries

Perhaps surprisingly, traditional craft upholstery doesn't involve a great deal of machine sewing. This is because sewing machines simply weren't widely available until the latter half of the nineteenth century and didn't become motorized until the twentieth century. Instead, much of the sewing is done by hand on the actual piece of furniture—so if traditional-style upholstery is the area you're intending to specialize in, a good-quality domestic sewing machine may be all you need for making up trims such as piping. However, if you're looking at working on more modern styles, or even creating unique one-off pieces of your own design, then it's worth investing in an industrial sewing machine. A domestic machine is designed to sew through fabrics that are much thinner than those commonly used in upholstery and even the longest available stitch length is frequently too short to create a really strong, durable seam.

Because of the cost of buying a brand-new machine, most people will opt for the second-hand route. I always recommend that you get a second-hand machine serviced by a specialist technician before you start using it, even if the buyer tells you that it's in perfect working order. The technician will also understand the workings of each machine and be able to advise you on needle sizes and types and suitable threads. Bear in mind

Sewing machine and accessories

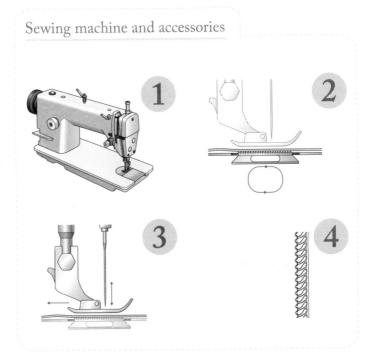

1 Flat-bed upholstery sewing machine

2 Base-feed machine

3 Walking-foot machine

4 Overlocking stitch

that industrial machines are table mounted and take up a lot of space compared to a domestic machine.

Here's a run-down of the features you should look for.

Flat-bed, post-bed, and cylinder-bed machines are all available, but for the vast majority of upholstery operations, a **flat-bed** is by far the most useful, simply because of the size of the bed.

There are both lock-stitch and chain-stitch machines: **lock-stitch** is the one you need. This is exactly the same stitch you find on domestic machines, where the needle enters the bed of the machine, picks up the bobbin thread, and takes it up to the top surface of the fabric, interlocking it with the top thread.

Next, look at the way the cloth is drawn through the machine – the "feed" mechanism. The most simple and widely available is a **base-feed** machine in which a single set of teeth beneath the machine plate feed around in a circular motion, pushing the fabric through the machine while the needle is making the stitches. This style of sewing machine will cope with most upholstery fabrics, but thicker fabrics, leather, and velvets may well require a **walking-foot** machine, in which the foot has two parts that move alternately so that one part of the foot is always clamping the fabric in place to prevent it from rucking or creeping. Even second-hand walking-foot machines can be as much as ten times the price of a base-feed machine, so they are more specialized pieces of kit aimed primarily at professionals.

Finally, how the machine is oiled is a key feature. I prefer a sewing machine that is oiled at key points as opposed to one that has an oil reservoir underneath from which the oil is drawn into the machine via a wick. The advantage of this is that, if you have to move the machine, there is less risk of spilling oil and ruining carpets or flooring. The downside is that you have to take care not to over-oil the machine head in case oil drips down onto the fabric being stitched.

All industrial sewing machines are designed to sew at speed, so when trying out an unfamiliar machine I recommend that you stitch some test pieces to get used to it. Apply only the very lightest pressure to the pedal, in much the same way that you would use the gas pedal on a car—using your toes rather than the full weight of your foot or leg.

Needles

Each brand and model of sewing machine will use a specified length of needle; your technician will be able to advise you. The two types of needle that I recommend for upholstery are round-point (designed for woven fabrics) and bayonet point, which is a specialist leather needle.

When fitting new needles, remember that on an industrial sewing machine the eye of the needle is threaded from left to right, whereas on domestic machines the thread runs from front to back. If, after fitting, the thread isn't catching around the bobbin, this is the first thing to check for.

Don't rely on just one bobbin: unlike a domestic machine, on an industrial machine you can thread a bobbin while you're sewing. There are several thread spools, so have thread from one reel threaded through the needle for sewing and thread from another reel being wound onto a spare bobbin for use as soon as it's needed. The mechanism for this is generally on the right-hand side of the machine and has a tension regulator similar to the one on the front of a domestic machine, ensuring even tension on the thread being wound onto the bobbin.

Serger or overlocker

A serger is a specialist type of sewing machine that has either three or five distinctive curved needles. It is used to bind the edges of a seam to prevent fraying where the seams will be rubbed or visible—for example, inside a loose cushion cover. A three-needle serger can also trim the seam allowance at the same time as it binds, to reduce bulk. A five-needle version does the same, and also applies a conventional lock stitch. Another use of sergers is to stabilize the outer edge of a fabric that may be prone to distorting or stretching while it is being sewn, in the same way that you might use a zigzag stitch on a domestic sewing machine. They are a useful addition to your tool set-up. Unlike domestic sewing machines, heavy-duty domestic sergers can cope with moderate use in upholstery, but if you're taking up upholstery seriously I would advise buying a second-hand industrial serger and having it serviced professionally.

Upholstery supplies and materials

Traditionally, upholstery sundry suppliers deal only with trade accounts, but increasingly there are retail outlets for the general public as well as online suppliers. The advantages of going to a retail outlet are that you can physically pick up the pieces and examine them, and also in many cases pick up invaluable bits of advice from the sales people. You can also buy small amounts of materials, whereas trade suppliers tend to deal in bulk. This section examines the range of specialist upholstery materials and fixings that you are likely to come across.

Tacks, nails, and staples

Tacks are used to hold woven materials such as webbing and fabrics such as burlap and linen; they are usually slightly faceted. Nails are used to attach fixings and fittings, such as serpentine spring clips (see page 120); they are made from round wire.

Upholstery tacks

Upholstery tacks are available in two basic forms. The first, which is broader at the head, is known as "improved," while the second, slimmer type is referred to as "fine." In general, tacks range in length from ¼" to 1" (6 mm to 25 mm). During their manufacture, the tacks are heat treated and cooled rapidly in a process designed to harden the metal, which accrues a bluish hue. Commonly these are known as "blued cut tacks."

Choosing which tack to use at which stage when upholstering is dictated by a number of factors. Principally, your tack choice will be determined by the dimensions of the rail and its condition. Understanding the strengths and weaknesses of the material being held in place by the tack will help you to make an informed choice as to which tack is appropriate. You should also take into account the differences between fine and improved tacks and the girth of the tack. As the diameter of fine tack heads is smaller, it fills less of the rail area—so by being economical with your tack use, there is less risk of buckling tacks by tapping them into tacks holding earlier layers in place.

Tacks that measure ⅝" (15 mm) are a cross between fine and improved tacks. They should only be used if the rail is thick and in good repair. Longer and thinner versions of this style of tack, often confused with upholstery tacks, are, in fact, better suited to carpet-laying.

Both fine and improved ½" (13-mm) tacks are used for a huge variety of everyday upholstery jobs. Improved ½" (13-mm) tacks are suitable for a range of processes, including fixing webbing, tacking burlap and fixing

Tacks, nails, and staples

1 Fine and
   improved tacks

2 Decorative
   upholstery nails

3 Staples

4 Gimp pins

cord lashings. Fine ½" (13-mm) tacks are better suited to performing the same functions on more delicate frames and run less risk of damaging the wood and finer fabrics. If the layer you're applying is load bearing, use an improved tack whenever possible.

Fine and improved ⅜" (10-mm) tacks have smaller heads than their ½" (13 mm) counterparts, so are better suited for use with finer frames and woven cloths. These two tacks work well when used in combination, temporary tacking with the larger-headed improved tacks and then refining the finish of the overall panel with fine tacks. More open-weave materials such as linen scrim may be too open for the smaller-headed ⅜" (10-mm) fine tacks, so in these instances using improved tacks should resolve the issue. However, if an improved ½" (13-mm) tack will either overhang the bevel and protrude from the frame or be set too far back into the pad in order to be flush at the front, trading up to a ½" (13-mm) fine tack may be the solution, as the head diameter of a ½" (13-mm) fine tack should be narrower than that of a ⅜" (10 mm)-improved tack.

Although they are used far less frequently, ¼" (6-mm) tacks are one of those supplies that are very handy on the very rare occasion you require them. Used principally for fixing very fine cloth over a minimum of batting, if any at all, they provide a fixing but very little bulk so they are ideal for tacking cloth to the edges of upholstered frames that sit snugly inside an outer frame.

Upholstery nails

Decorative upholstery nails come in many sizes, shapes and colors, ranging from small, traditional antique nails through to large, glittery, faceted crystal. The vast majority of nails applied to furniture have a domed head and diameter of around ⅜" (1 cm). Available in dozens of finishes, they can be set into the wood, butting up against each other to form a continuous line or evenly spaced. They are used to great effect where upholstery finishes against show wood. In commercial upholstery a faster method has evolved, referred to as "strip nails"; these 3-feet (1-meter) lengths look like a line of decorative nails but they only require a nail to be placed once for every five nail heads.

Staples

The most universally available staple size suitable for upholstery is referred to as 71 series. The staples are made from an alloy wire that is about ¹⁄₁₆" (1 mm) thick. The staple crown is just under ⅜" (10 mm) wide, and the prongs range from ⅛" to ⅝" (4 mm to 16 mm) long. However, some upholsterers prefer the 53 series staples and the guns required to fire them. A 53 series staple is made from thicker wire than the 71 type, which means that it doesn't shoot through leather and vinyl as readily.

Both types of staple are effective but I do think that they lend themselves to different applications. In my opinion, the slim prongs of the 71 series staple are much better for firing into hardwood frames and hard/dense board materials, whereas the 53 series staples are less likely to cut through delicate fabric or vinyl or bite too firmly into foam. I have also found that the galvanized amalgam used to make 53 series staples is less likely to corrode as fast as the 71s. Fully stainless-steel staples are available for both crown sizes, but they do come at around ten times the price per box.

The longest staples that will fit into an upholstery staple gun's magazine are ⁹⁄₁₆" (14-mm) staples, which are used in place of ⅝" (15-mm) tacks. Effective when fired into softer wood frames, they will also penetrate most hardwoods but will probably buckle if fired into very hard composite board materials or dry antique hardwood rails. They are a bit of a mixed blessing, because they are easy to put in but can really take some patience to extract.

For a bridging length between ⅜" (10-mm) and ⁹⁄₁₆" (14-mm) staples, ⁷⁄₁₆" (12-mm) staples grip well enough into softwood rails and through thicker fabrics that ⅜" (10-mm) staples can't clamp over; they are also less likely than ⁹⁄₁₆" (14-mm) staples to buckle when fired into a hard substrate.

The most commonly used staple length is ⅜" (10 mm); this has pretty much replaced ⅜" (10-mm) and ½" (13-mm) tacks for most operations, even for those such as myself, who have a fondness for tacks.

Traditional black-and-white webbing, jute webbing, elasticated webbing, rubber webbing, and polypropylene webbing

Gimp pins

Colored gimp pins are pretty much the smallest nails used in upholstery. Named as they are, gimp pins are principally used in the application of gimp and braid to a finished piece of furniture. They are also extremely useful for attaching fabric to a frame and their color allows them to blend into fabrics or, more increasingly, to be used to make a feature.

Webbing

Prior to the introduction of pre-fabricated spring units, webbing was the first layer of most upholstered pads and still provides the first suspension layer in most upholstery. There are various kinds, and your choice will be dictated partly by the cost involved and partly on where on the piece of furniture the pad is being built (a seat requires a heavier-duty, stronger webbing than an arm, for example). Another factor is whether or not you will need to stitch through the webbing. You can stitch through jute webbing, for example, but not through rubber and elasticated webbing. Webbing tends to be a standard weight, so if you need to make the webbing more resilient, space the webs closer together. The width of webbing varies from country to country: in the United States and France, webbing tends to be 2½" (6 cm) wide, whereas in the United Kingdom it is 2" (5 cm) wide.

For more information on attaching webbing, turn to page 107.

Black-and-white webbing

Traditional black-and-white webbing, woven in a herringbone twill, has a deep-rooted affinity with British upholstery. Originally it was made solely from flax, which was abundant during the eighteenth century. Nowadays, it is generally made from a combination of jute and linen. It is the most expensive natural webbing. It comes in one standard width of 2" (5 cm).

Jute webbing

The most common form of webbings used in upholstery worldwide are made from jute. Herringbone twill versions are available, but most are woven more simply. Available principally in widths of 2" and 3" (5 cm and 7.5 cm) widths, the weight-bearing capacity of jute webbing is similar to that of black-and-white webbing, but it is considerably cheaper. It can be used under a traditional stuffed pad and under foam.

Elasticated webbing

Elasticated webbing is, as its name suggests, designed to stretch. Varying degrees of stretch are achieved, depending on how the elastic is woven. Very conveniently, it is sold in varying percentages of elasticity. The general rule is that the lower the percentage of elastic, the less stretch the webbing will have. However, using wider elasticated webbings will also affect a webbing's performance by increasing the tension. Only use elasticated webbing under a foam pad.

Rubber webbing

Rubber webbing, manufactured exclusively for the upholstery industry by Pirelli for many years, is made from vulcanized latex rubber and is the predecessor of elasticated webbing. Still available today, this typically beige webbing is widely regarded as the premium product to span a frame with when flexible webbings are required. It can be fixed to a frame using a wide variety of methods and fittings, from stapling directly onto the wooden frame to using fixings made up from multiple components to suspend the webbing between metal frames. It was widely used by furniture manufacturer Ercol in the second half of the twentieth century as the suspension layer of a seat, with a cushion simply placed on top; however, it can also be used inside a pad. Its limitation is that it perishes in saline air, so its lifespan is dramatically reduced in coastal areas.

Polypropylene webbing

Made from a woven plastic, polypropylene webbing is used for masking edges in contract upholstery and in the place of jute webbing in large-scale, batch-produced furniture.

Springs

For more information on attaching springs, turn to page 115.

Prior to the development of springs, upholstery padding was a little limited in its ability to provide comfort. Sure enough, the padding-over-webbing format had served the craft well, but with time, webbing alone will stretch and hair fillings will compact, creating the well-used dip in older seats bemoaned by diners and loved by cats.

The springs that we know today were first patented early in the nineteenth century. Spring wire needs to be very durable, but also to have the ability to flex and return to its original place. This is achieved by work hardening (strengthening) the steel wire by drawing or extruding it through ever-decreasing widths of dies. To reduce the likelihood of corrosion or rusting, a thin layer of copper is then applied, but strength is ultimately determined by the thickness of the wire. Including carbon in the steel manufacturing process hardens some springs that have tightly wound coils of wire and as a result cannot be made from a gauge of wire that is too thick.

Although you will probably only be replacing worn springs with new ones of the same type, basing your choice of spring solely on appearance

Springs

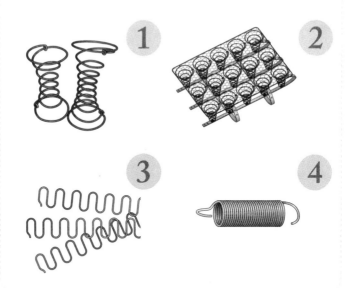

won't necessarily give the best outcome. Only by compressing the spring and getting a feel for the flex will you be able to ascertain which combination of spring height and gauge of wire is correct. If you change the springing method for something different, make sure that the spring style and method of fixing it to the frame will load stress in a way that is compatible with how the frame is constructed.

The **double-cone spring** has a classic hour-glass shape that is typically associated with traditional upholstery techniques, although it has many modern applications. Taller, thicker springs tend to work best in seats, whereas springs of medium height and gauge are better for chair backs, and arms and headrests typically require smaller, thinner springs. The invention of the double-cone spring changed day-to-day upholstery forever. Instead of the more sculptural process of stuffing, regulating and stitching, the volume of a pad could be dictated by selecting the desired height and gauge of spring, stitching the springs to webs tacked onto the rails, lashing them in place with laid cord, and closing off with a layer of burlap. Softer and wider pads could be fitted over the sprung base and the sitter was elevated to a level of comfort experienced by very few until that point.

Mesh-top spring units are pre-manufactured units made with single-cone springs. A mesh-top unit is supported by a lattice of metal laths nailed onto a wooden frame or wound around a metal rail and riveted or welded to the rail. Due to the flexing of frames, welds weaken and break fairly rapidly, so most metal frames or sprung metal components require specialist fabrication. A completed unit still needs to be lashed into place, but in my experience it can more than halve the time it takes to construct a hand-sprung unit.

Serpentine springs are distinctive in appearance and flex in a completely different way to coiled springs. Also known as zigzag springs because of their distinctive shape, serpentine springs are usually attached directly to just two rails and held to the frame with one of several specially devised spring clips. Lashings, anchor ties, or wire, and clips hold the rows of serpentine springs parallel to one another. Choosing the length of spring to use is a particular skill: thinner springs will obviously stretch more than springs made using a heavier gauge of wire, but in longer spans the difference will be multiplied, so on occasion you will need to choose a heavier-gauge wire than was first intended. Designed for speed of fitting

Selecting the right gauge of spring

Until you're an experienced upholsterer, it's likely that you'll be re-upholstering existing pieces rather than upholstering a new piece of furniture from scratch. This means that the decision on which type of spring to use will already have been made—so if the springs are badly worn and you can't re-use them, all you have to do is replace like for like. However, you will need to use springs of differing degrees of firmness, depending on the density of pad that you want and where the springs are situated. The thicker the wire from which the spring is made, the firmer the pad will be. (Confusingly, the thicker the wire, the lower the gauge number.) The chart below is a guide to what to use.

Part being upholstered	Firmness required	Gauge of wire	Available spring lengths
Headrest/ Armrest	Soft/medium	13-gauge	4–8" (10–20 cm)
	Firm	12-gauge	3–9" (7.5–23 cm)
Back	Soft	12-gauge	3–9" (7.5–23 cm)
	Medium	11-gauge	3–7" (7.5–17.5 cm)
	Firm	10-gauge	3–9" (7.5–23 cm)
Seat	Soft	11-gauge	3–7" (7.5–17.5 cm)
	Medium	10-gauge	3–9" (7.5–23 cm)
	Firm	9- or 8.5-gauge	3–12" (7.5–30 cm

and for use in thin seat pads, they are synonymous with budget furniture. They can be purchased in either pre-cut lengths of around 15–30" (38–75 cm) or bought as a roll and cut to the required length using bolt cutters or a guillotine.

Serpentine springs fitted individually load an enormous amount of force into frames and the frame is constantly under tension, so they really are better suited to frames of a solid hardwood construction. Because of this, it is not uncommon to see frame rails that have been bent or twisted. For this reason, I tend to prefer to use **serpentine spring units**, which have a flexible edge and load less stress into a frame. More commonly known as a fish-mouth unit because of the gaping appearance of the front edge, these units address the flexing at the front edge under the sitter's knee rather than simply flexing in the center of the seat, thus more closely mimicking the performance of a coil spring. Super-loop zigzag springs are made with much broader loops than the thicker-gauge seat types and tend to be used in backs and arms. Despite feeling much softer, they hold their shape well and can be used to great effect in speeding up arm and back springing under a variety of filling types.

Often found on mid-nineteenth-century wing and armchairs, **tension springs** made it possible to span sleek frames with the minimum of stress to the frame and avoid bulk in the upholstery. They are made from tightly wound coils of carbon steel. As the name suggests, this type of spring performs by being under constant tension. Typically, spring lengths range from 14–20" (35–50 cm). You can increase the tension by choosing a much shorter length than the gap you intend to span or slacken off the spring by reducing the stretch and choosing a slightly longer length of spring. They are manufactured in three thicknesses, one (the thickest) for seats and two for backs. Each of those thicknesses can be made in different gauges of wire, and you would generally choose a thicker gauge for areas that bear more weight or need more support. Tension springs can be fixed to the frame in a variety of ways, from using standard fittings to hand-made solutions, nails, and netting staples. The coiled nature of the spring allows it to bear load in a similar way to a serpentine spring, but the flexing is very different and far less stressful for the frame. Originally, the coils of the tension spring were sheathed in a woven textile similar to climbing rope or a Chinese finger trap, but over the last 20 years or so this has been replaced by plastic sheathing. The sheath is important to the performance of the spring because, without it, the spring could bite into the fabric and degrade a pad from the inside as it flexes. Another advantage of the sheathing is that the springs can be fitted to an open frame without looking unfinished.

Burlap and linen scrim

Woven materials

Virtually every stage of upholstery uses woven textiles of one kind or another. The heaviest of these lie deep down in the pad, perhaps covering webbings or springs. Thick and tightly woven, they are a barrier that protects the stuffing above from being worn out by the suspension system below. As we move up through successive layers of the pad, we move on to more loosely woven linen scrim, followed by muslin (calico) and robust platform fabrics. In essence, woven materials denote the changes in the upholstery while preventing the various suspension systems and fillings from merging into one and losing shape.

Burlap is the real workhorse of woven materials. It is generally the first cloth layer and keeps the suspension system contained while providing even support for ties that will hold the spring tops in place and a base for stuffing ties (see page 155). Lighter burlaps can be laid over stuffings and stitched to form firm pads or used over loose fillings in thin pads. Burlap is woven using fibers harvested from the stem of the jute plant and is available in various weights and widths. The three weights available are approximately 7½ oz, 10 oz, and 12 oz (200 grams, 280 grams, and 340 grams). When considering which weight of burlap is appropriate for each stage of your upholstery, be guided by the openness of the weave— the deeper you are into the foundation of the upholstered pad, the heavier the weave should be. For example, it would be unwise to cover springs with 7½-oz (200-gram) burlap.

Scrim serves exactly the same purpose as burlap. Traditionally, it was made from either flax or linen, although flax has been replaced by jute. Jute scrim looks very similar to burlap, but you can tell the difference between them by pulling a few strands of fiber out and assessing whether they appear flattened and crimped (scrim) or rounded and wavy (burlap). Unfortunately, linen scrims come with a considerably higher price tag than the more widely available jute. Whether or not the cost is justifiable is purely down to individual upholsterers, but I use it for stitching first stuffings whenever possible. It is second to none for stitching fine-detailed pads, but it requires a softer and more skilled hand to work it than jute burlap or scrim.

Muslin (calico) is a woven cotton cloth that is widely used in many crafts. Upholstery applications for this fabric range from encasing soft fibers while still allowing them to be puffy to being pulled very tight over coarse fillings and tacked down hard onto the frame. It is also available in a form that has been impregnated with fire-retardant chemicals. Known as calico barrier cloth, this layer can be used directly under non-fire-retardant fabrics to ensure they comply with fire regulations.

Like muslin (calico), **platform fabric** is woven from cotton. Because it is dyed in a choice of colors and is durable it can be used in a variety of roles, from backing cloths to more load-bearing operations. The surface of platform cloth is generally flat. Bolton twill is a type of platform lining that has a stronger weave, made evident by the distinctive diagonal pattern. Synthetic platform cloths are manufactured in a variety of colors, textures and degrees of stretch; they are frequently used in lower-quality, high-volume upholstery.

Ticking is a very robust cotton lining material with a distinctive striped appearance and traditionally it was used to cover mattresses. Less commonly used these days as part of a chair's upholstery other than in some areas of traditional craft upholstery, it remains widely available and is an excellent material to use where a lot of strength is required from a thin and relatively inexpensive material.

As the name suggests, **bottoming cloth** is used principally to dress the underside of a chair to mask the loose ends and cut fibers often visible when a chair is upturned. Nowadays, the cotton-mix weave is usually looser than that of platform cloth; as a result, bottoming cloth really isn't suitable for any load-bearing applications. Generally available in only black, it is tightly woven enough to catch dust as the upholstered seat degrades with age and use—hence its other name of dust cloth.

Woven polypropylene is used in contract upholstery and factory-produced domestic upholstery to line the underside of upholstered pieces and the outsides of panels prior to the outside covers being fitted. As it is prone to fraying while being handled, it must be applied with generous turnings.

Waxed cambric receives a very fine, waxed treatment to increase its resilience to puncturing without stiffening it too much. This makes it an excellent choice for encasing feathers in loose cushions and fixed upholstered feather back pads.

Muslin (calico), platform fabric, ticking, bottoming cloth and waxed cambric.

Laid cord, sisal, upholstery twine, nylon twine and slipping thread.

Threads, cords, and twines

There are various kinds of twine used in upholstery to bind the layers of the pad together. The heavier the materials that you're locking in place, the heavier the twine you need to use. Some twines are made from natural fibers; nylon twine is also available. As your physical strength as an upholsterer develops, you may need to vary the type you're using so that you are not constantly snapping it through using too much force. As you get toward the final stages of building the pad, you will need to use slipping thread to hand stitch panels of fabric together.

Laid cord is the heaviest cord or thread used in upholstery and differs in construction from most conventional twisted natural-fiber cords. The flax or hemp fibers are flattened out, stretched and then matted together with a light twist. Due to the pithy nature of the fibers, they clump together fairly easily, so only minimal twist is required to form the finished thickness. The principal advantage of not twisting the fibers is that they do not stretch when under tension or form loops when tying knots. Laid cord needs to be robust, as its main use is for lashing heavy-gauge springs to the frame. A greater choice of laid cord thicknesses has been a relatively recent development and upholsterers have a greater selection than ever before. Thinner laid cords are suited to delicate-gauge wire springs such as back and arm springs—as the gauge increases, so should the thickness and durability of the laid cord.

Sisal is derived from the agave plant. Unlike laid cord, the fibers are twisted together into a rope-like construction. It is much coarser than laid cord and can be quite tough on your hands. Its popularity is due principally to its cost, as it is much cheaper than laid cord. It also offers a natural material for people who do not want to use a nylon cord. It's slightly thinner than the thickest laid cord. It can be used for all the same applications as laid cord, but it is less durable. Due to its twisted nature, it will stretch slightly over time.

Constructed with a twisted combination of flax and hemp, **traditional upholstery twine** is available in three thicknesses: 3-cord is simply three strands twisted together, 4-cord is constructed from four strands and 6-cord has six strands. Six-cord twine is used principally for tying the 12-oz (340-gram) burlap layer to the springs and for stuffing ties (see page 155). The 3- and 4-cord twines are used for edge-stitching techniques (see page 169). When deciding which one to use, you need to balance the thickness of the twine, the length of stitch required, and the needle you have chosen. Traditionally, upholsterers draw the length of twine through a block of hard beeswax to make it easier to slide through the materials (see page 169).

Nylon twine is used for the same purposes as traditional upholstery twine. As thin as 3-cord twine but more resilient than 6-cord, it is longer lasting than traditional twine and inherently lubricated. It slides through upholstered pads and is the most adaptable twine by a long way. Many traditional upholsterers will not use it for edge-stitching techniques, as it can slip and loosen with time. You will also come across nylon buttoning twine, in which the strands are slightly fused together so that, when you cut it, they do not spring apart in the same way as ordinary nylon twine; for that reason, I prefer it to conventional nylon twine.

Usually made from fine linen, **slipping threads** are used primarily for hand sewing borders and outside panels closed. They are either bleached white or dyed to one of many colors. Curiously, new threads are still sold in skeins, although they are more frequently supplied on reels—but twines sold by the reel are more likely to have extra twist in them and to gather into small knots during fine stitching. Traditionally, these threads are waxed to make it easier to pull them through tough fabrics; however, I advise against this unless you are experienced enough to know whether the wax will build up on the fabric being sewn and discolor the holes made by the needle. Heavier, polished threads are occasionally suited for upholstery use, but the thickness of the thread is limited by the range of needles with a big enough eye.

Upholstery fillings and battings

Fillings are used on top of suspension systems (webbing and/or springs). They define the shape and volume of the pad and prevent the sitter from feeling the springs beneath. How densely the filling is packed will determine the softness of the pad. Batting layers are much thinner, and are used on top of the burlap or scrim layers that cover the filling to prevent it from migrating out of the pad through the fabric; they also offer the upholsterer a final opportunity to add volume and define shape before the top cover is put on.

Experienced upholsterers can pretty much stuff most things into a plethora of shapes and attach them to a multitude of frame shapes— so rather than attempt to catalogue absolutely everything you might encounter in day-to-day upholstery, I'm going to look at a selection of key stuffing materials in some depth.

Loose, natural fillings

Seaweeds, grasses, mosses, hay, straw—almost any natural fiber you can think of will, at some point, have been used as an upholstery filling, depending on what materials are available locally. Loose fillings used

Coir, horsetail hair, foam, and reconstituted foam.

nowadays in upholstery include natural plant fibers and various kinds of animal hair. They are sold by weight and are used in traditional craft upholstery, but due to the labor-intensive nature of working them and the cost of the materials, they are no longer found in most new domestic furniture. The key feature of fiber processing that appears to make a fiber perform exceptionally well is the introduction of twists to the fibers, enabling efficient storage and transportation. This also results in a loose coil being taken up by the fiber, which in turn gives the best fibers a springiness that lasts for a considerable length of time.

Coir fiber used in upholstery is generally a by-product of the coconut industry. The fibers that are of greatest interest are the longer fibers that make up the bulk of the nut's protection during growth; fully mature coconuts provide the most resilient fiber. Ginger coir fiber is available treated with fire retardants or untreated and offers the best value to the majority of upholsterers. Black fiber is simply coir that has been dyed; the treatment coagulates in drying and results in this version of coir being less dusty when being prepared for stuffing than its ginger counterpart. With careful preparation and application, coir stuffing can last within a well-constructed pad for generations.

The use of **cattle hair** in upholstery has fluctuated; currently its use is in the ascendant principally due to its cost compared to horsehair. Usually white or gray in color, its natural softness is enhanced by washing and light bleaching. On occasion it is supplied as part of a general mix of cattle, horse and hog hairs.

Horse mane and pig hair mix combines the two fibers into a widely available hair filling. The two fibers lack the length of tail hairs, resulting in a less springy filling that compacts easily.

Horsetail hair can only be described as the "Rolls Royce" of stuffings. This once readily available stuffing has declined in use and the hair used nowadays is principally a by-product of the meat-processing industry, with fewer companies involved in its preparation for upholstery use. Long tail-hair strands can reach a good 2 feet (60 cm) in length. Once the fibers have been washed and chemically treated, they are twisted and then dried and baled. Once cut and carded, the strands rest into loose coils, which offer fantastic properties for shaping and molding soft yet substantial upholstered pads. Unfortunately, horsetail hair is around eight times more expensive than coir fiber. More often than not, horsetail hair is now used as a second stuffing over the top of a pad constructed from a cheaper filling. Its springy, lofty nature means that it is suited to softening the top of a pad constructed from cheaper, denser fibers.

Sheet material fillings

The principal advantage of using a sheet material as a filling is the consistent thickness and density, so building up a pad's thickness can be done in a very systematic way. Sheet materials are quicker to use as fillings than loose materials; they also require less technical skill, so are a good starting point for complete beginners. Both manmade and natural sheet material fillings are available.

Foam was first discovered by a scientist working for DuPont in the mid-1930s, but wasn't widely used in furniture constructions until the mid-1950s. It is produced in large blocks that are then cut into sheet form in standard thicknesses and can be carved into almost any shape you wish. By changing the chemical formula, the density of foam can be varied to

Selecting the right density of foam

Foam is available in different densities and each density tends to be manufactured in one specific color for ease of identification. Although this system is not completely standardized worldwide, most suppliers will understand what you mean if you ask for "soft" or "white" foam, for example. Note, however, that if foam is exposed to UV light for a prolonged period, the color will be affected, making it slightly harder to identify the grade by sight alone.

The chart below sets out which grade of foam would be suitable for different parts of a piece of furniture, depending on the level of firmness you are looking for.

Part being upholstered	Firmness required	Grade of foam	Color
Headrest/armrest	Soft	RX21	White
	Medium	RX24	Lilac or gray
	Firm	RX33	Green
Back	Soft	RX24	Lilac or gray
	Medium	RX33	Green
	Firm	RX39	Blue
Seat	Soft	RG50	Pink or orange
	Medium	RX39	Blue
	Medium–soft, better performance	RG50 over RX39	Pink over blue
	Firm	RX39 over reconstituted foam	Blue over multicolor

Note: By combining different densities of foam, you can maintain the softness but increase the longevity of the cushion by giving it a firmer core.

*Latex rubber sheeting, rubberized hair, horsehair
on burlap, white cotton felt*

suit different applications, from very soft foams used in headboards, for example, to very dense foams used in seats on public transport. The foam companies all use different codes and colors to denote the foam density.

Reconstituted foam is made by breaking scraps of waste foam into crumbs that are then compressed into blocks. The amount of pressure per square inch used to compress the foam determines its density, so a 12-lb (5.4-kg) reconstituted foam is considerably more dense than a 5-lb (2.25-kg) foam. Really heavy, dense foams are quite specialized materials and not something that most amateurs will encounter.

The raw rubber used to manufacture natural **latex rubber sheeting** is tapped from trees in the traditional way, which means that the density cannot be varied in the same way as that of foam. This has to be done mechanically by creating air pockets within the sheet—leading to its most common name, pin-core latex—which egulates both the density and the weight of the rubber. Very popular in the first half of the twentieth century, its use then declined due mainly to the cost of production and its inherent weight. It is, however, becoming more popular again as people look for natural alternatives to foam-based products. It can be carved in similar ways to foam but you would need a specialist cutter.

Rubberized hair or **coir sheeting** is enjoying a revival in popularity. Constructed from 40% natural latex and 60% mixed hair and coir, these products are becoming increasingly used as a sustainable upholstery filling material. Available in thicknesses of 1" and 2" (2.5 cm and 5 cm), rubberized sheets can be molded over the top of loose stuffings, secured to the frame, tied and stitched to make a soft pad. Early on as an apprentice, I realized that this was one of the few natural materials that allowed upholsterers to speed up traditional processes and retain the natural-fiber element of upholstery, rather than simply turn to manmade foams when looking to minimize labor.

Burlap-backed fillings
Coir on burlap and **hog hair on burlap** combine the ease and convenience of sheet materials with the feel of traditional loose fillings. Although they're not common, they are a good compromise for both amateur and professional upholsterers who want to create the look and feel of a traditional filling without the prohibitive material costs of loose natural fillings or the labor time required to apply them.

Batting
There are both natural and manmade battings. In the past, natural battings tended to be cotton based, but wool battings are now becoming more readily available and their resilience is improving.

White cotton felt is made from waste produced during the process of refining cotton fiber to make fabric. This fluffy, unbleached batting is generally around 1" (2.5 cm) thick and is excellent for both preventing strong fibers contained within the pad from migrating as well as for adding volume in an even and consistent way.

Wool/cotton-mix felt has developed to comply with recent changes in legislation across Europe banning the use of bromides at the levels that were once required to make the filling comply with fire regulations. The result is a slightly lighter batting than the 100% cotton felt and it is a little more prone to falling apart while being dressed into place. Overall, this product is still more than suitable for all upholstery applications where the use of cotton felt is appropriate.

Needled rag felt is denser than the cotton batting but, unlike the burlap-backed products, it is strong enough to hold itself together. Recycled fibers make up the batting, giving it a dark, multicolored appearance. Usually applied early in pad construction, it is excellent for reducing the impact of springs wearing a seat away from the inside or softening a wooden rail where minimal upholstery is required.

Layered rag felt is similar to needled rag felt in composition, but the overall result is a much fluffier and wispier batting. Used in conjunction with denser felts and/or rubberized sheets, this batting offers an effective way of bulking out a pad with a soft layer manufactured from recycled materials.

Black felt bonded onto Typar (Typar is a manmade, heat-bonded fabric) is a stiffer and heavier style of batting, due to the process that bonds the Typar to the felt. The backing is very robust and will cope with abrasion relatively well over small areas and it can be used as a single layer directly over springs. The backing also enables the batting to be fixed easily to a frame with either staples or spray adhesive.

Black felt bonded on to typar

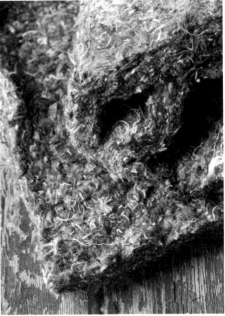

Needled rag felt

Polyester batting

Layered rag felt

Traditional skin batting is increasingly difficult to source and no doubt will become all but obsolete once well-treasured stocks of the material have diminished. This thin batting comprises a core of cotton felt that is coated on both sides with a flat layer of starch forming the "skin." In traditional upholstery skin batting was used just under the top cover, as it added a degree of softness and prevented the strong fibers inside the pad from migrating through the cover. Since the decline in its manufacture, alternatives have been developed using a combination of wool and thin, manmade fibers that perform relatively closely to the original skin batting.

Polyester batting is thermally bonded in a similar way to Typar, but it is much looser and fluffier. It is graded by weight—the higher the number, the thicker the batting. For example, 2-oz (50-gram) batting (the thinnest available) is under ⅜" (1 cm) thick, while 14-oz (400-gram) (the thickest commonly available) is around 1¼" (3 cm) thick. Unlike cotton batting, this is so open that it won't prevent fillings from migrating through. However, a benefit of this open structure is that it's super fluffy and offers a lightness to the touch that no other filling can offer. You can glue layers together with spray adhesive to make thicker layers if required. Regardless of whether I'm working on a modern, foam-filled construction or a traditional piece, this is my preferred layer for placing directly under the top cover. There is also a loose version of polyester batting known as hollow-fill fiber that is commonly used as a cushion filling. Because the strands tend to mat and felt together, it does need to be regularly teased apart and so is not suitable for use in an area of upholstery that is not easily accessible.

Skin batting

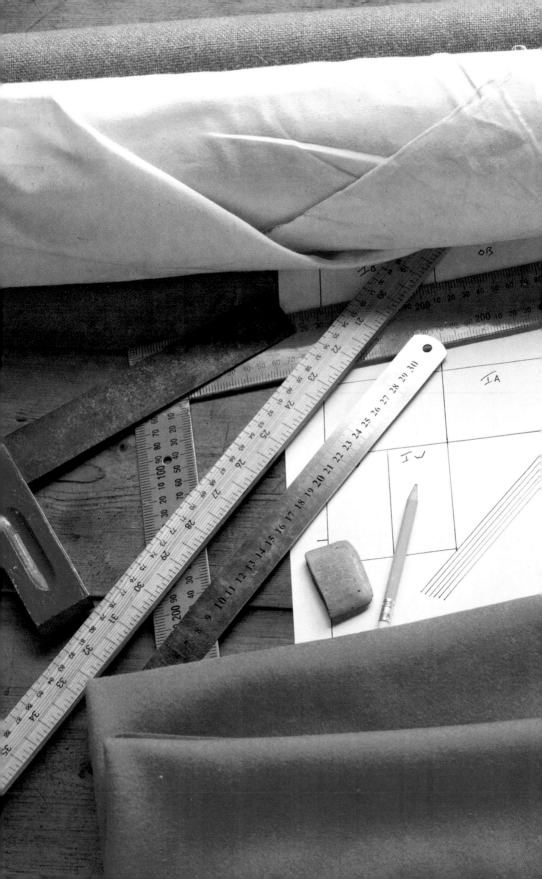

Before you start

Chapter 2

Before you start

Frame styles and construction

Most upholstered frames tend to be constructed from either wood or metal (although polystyrene, fiberglass and plastic have all played a part in frame making). Here's a quick look at five common frame styles in order of difficulty and complexity. Although you don't need to know exactly how the piece was made, it's worth knowing what the individual parts are called, as these are terms that crop up all the time in upholstery and they provide a useful "shorthand" way of describing the area that you're working on. You will find blueprint methods on pages 224–249, detailing both modern and traditional processes required to upholster each frame style.

Jargon buster

Drop-in: A pad that is upholstered and drops into or fits onto a non-upholstered frame.

Stuffover: In a stuffover seat, a traditional webbing is applied to the top of a rail and then a stitched, upholstered pad is constructed and fixed to the top of that rail. The covering is either then tacked off under the frame or fixed and trimmed on the face of the rails.

Sprung stuffover: The webbing is applied to the underside of the rail, and a spring is then fitted that is deeper than the rail. Once the springs are secured, a pad is constructed in a similar way to a stuffover pad.

Drop-in seat

This is the starting point for most people in upholstery and involves creating a separate upholstered pad that sits inside the shell of the frame. This style of upholstery is limited in that you cannot build much volume into the pad; the depth of the pad is determined by the thickness of the seat rail.

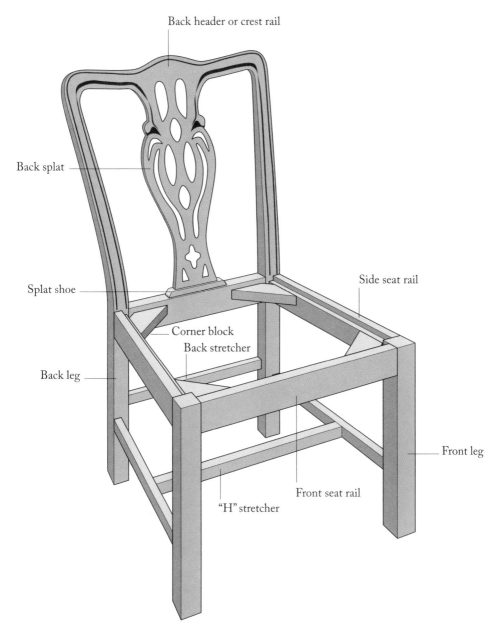

Back header or crest rail

Back splat

Splat shoe

Side seat rail

Corner block

Back stretcher

Back leg

Front leg

"H" stretcher

Front seat rail

Stuffover and sprung stuffover pads

A stuffover pad sits on top of the frame and has a much thicker layer of stuffing than a drop-in style. The stuffing is secured in place and formed to make an edge that matches the profile of the frame, using various stitching techniques (see page 169). A sprung stuffover pad uses similar stuffing and stitching techniques, but it sits over springs. In upholstery terms, this is the next stage of complexity beyond the drop-in seat.

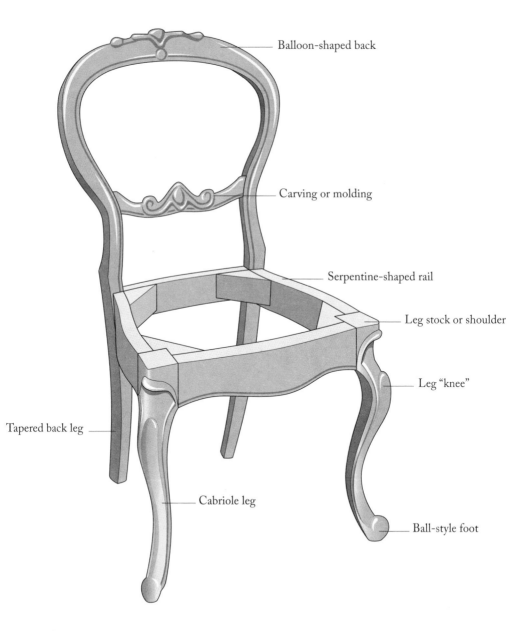

Balloon-shaped back

Carving or molding

Serpentine-shaped rail

Leg stock or shoulder

Leg "knee"

Tapered back leg

Cabriole leg

Ball-style foot

Tub chair

In a typical tub chair, the back and arms are upholstered as well as the seat. This gives you a good opportunity to master varying the density and thickness of the stuffing, as different pads on the chair require differing levels of firmness. (The back and arms, for example, will be softer and often thinner than the seat.) You will also have to get to grips with manipulating upholstery around the curve of the chair.

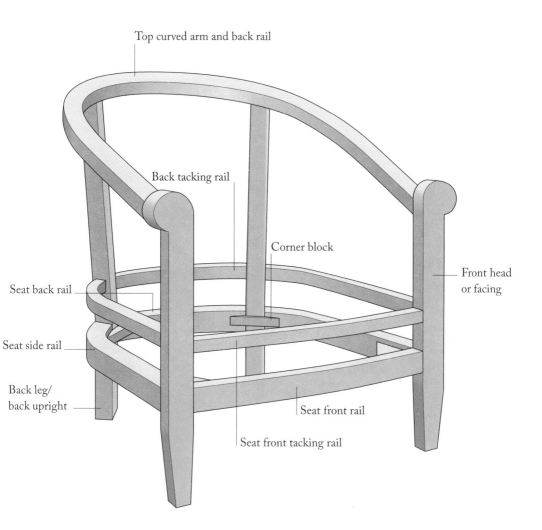

Top curved arm and back rail

Back tacking rail

Corner block

Front head
or facing

Seat back rail

Seat side rail

Back leg/
back upright

Seat front rail

Seat front tacking rail

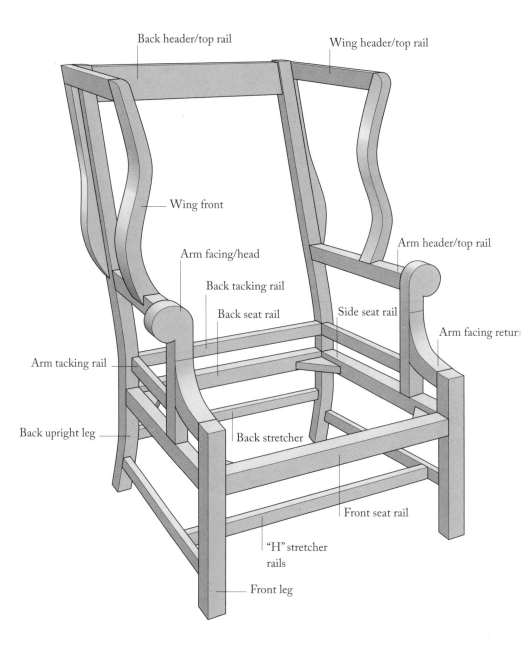

Back header/top rail

Wing header/top rail

Wing front

Arm facing/head

Arm header/top rail

Back tacking rail

Back seat rail

Side seat rail

Arm facing return

Arm tacking rail

Back upright leg

Back stretcher

Front seat rail

"H" stretcher rails

Front leg

Wing chair

Wing chairs are more complicated shapes, with a greater number of panels to upholster. On the back alone, there are three main sections: the lumbar section, the main area of the back, and the headrest. All these sections require a similar treatment; however, the density and the thickness of the stuffing will vary from one area to another, yet it must still look like a single coherent piece. You will also have to contend with keeping the pattern of the fabric running consistently across several different pads, some of which (for example, the wings) may be on a different plane from an adjacent pad (the back).

A wing chair prepared for re-covering.

Upholstery fabrics

There are lots of different upholstery fabrics on the market—brocade, chintz, traditional tapestries, and those with a modern take, to name but a few—but the most important thing to consider is whether or not the fabric you like the look of is hard-wearing enough for its intended purpose. The structure of the fabric is generally tested for its resistance to wear, using a test known as the Martindale or (more commonly) rub test, while the dyes are tested for light- and colorfastness. Fabrics are also often tested both dry and wet to see if they can withstand spillages.

In a rub test, a small sample of the fabric is continuously rubbed from front to back or from side to side by a machine to simulate the wear to which it would be subjected in normal use. Each country or region has very few approved testing centers, so that consistent results are achieved. When you buy upholstery fabrics, you will find that they are generally referred to in terms of the number of rubs that they can withstand. This information should be contained within every fabric swatch book and may be given as either a number of rubs or as a general classification such as "suitable for light domestic use."

The number of rubs for different categories of use is not set in stone, but the figures below are based on my experience of the way fabric manufacturers classify their products.

Light domestic use	13–15,000 rubs
General domestic use	about 25,000 rubs
Heavy domestic use	over 30,000 rubs
General contract use	40–50,000 rubs
Severe contract use	75,000 rubs and above

Estimating fabric amounts

When you're re-upholstering, always measure for new fabric before you rip down and remove the old. If you take off the old fabric before measuring, it's very difficult to know how much fabric you need to allow for the depth of the pad. My students often ask me why they can't just take off the old fabric and measure it. Existing covers are useful as a guide, but there are several reasons why you can't rely entirely on those dimensions: you may be changing the volume of the pad; the existing cover will have been trimmed after it has been tacked in place, so following those dimensions might mean that you cut a piece too small to allow yourself to stretch it tight over the rail or fillings; and different fabrics have different elasticity, due to the composition of the fibers or the way they have been woven, so they may have stretched. And if the size of the pattern repeat on the fabric you're planning to use is dramatically different from the original, this can have a huge bearing on both the size of the panel that you cut and where you place that panel on the roll of fabric.

When you're estimating, err slightly on the generous side to allow for things like the seat or back pad having sagged. You will also need to take into account things like seam allowances (if pieces of fabric are stitched together) and the depth of the rail if fabric is to be tacked down (you need not only enough to tack down but also enough to be able to pull the fabric and hold it in place while you tack).

Professional tip

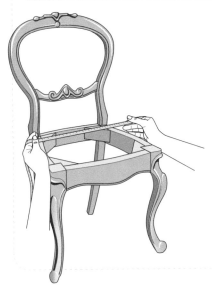

If you buy a bare frame with no previous stuffing, place an off-cut of foam over each panel and measure over that rather than just taking a flat measurement across each panel. Alternatively, stretch the tape measure over your hands to estimate the depth of the pad.

Taking measurements

Use a flexible tape measure rather than a fixed steel ruler, as this allows you to follow the contours of the pad. Also, although steel tape measures are the preferred tool for very rough estimates, they tend to bend or kink when you take them over a curve, so it's difficult to get a completely accurate measurement.

Measure each individual panel and make a note of the measurements so that you can mark them on a cutting plan (see page 79), remembering to allow for seam allowances and stretching fabric over the rail.

The diagrams opposite show where to take measurements on the four basic frame styles described earlier. In each case, add on the depth of the pad all around, plus a generous 2" (5 cm) all around each panel to allow for turnings.

These measurements will tell you the size of each individual panel of fabric that you need to cut. However, you can't just add them all together to work out how much fabric you need to buy. This is because you need to take into account the size of any pattern repeat and pattern placement.

Professional tip

If you're short of fabric, or using a very expensive fabric, you won't want to waste any! At the edges of the panel—where the fabric's going to be hidden under, say, an arm—top stitch (see page 177) a piece of similar-weight but less expensive fabric to extend the width or length. This is generally referred to as a "fly." When you're upholstering a whole suite of furniture or a large piece such as a sofa, this can end up saving you several yards of fabric.

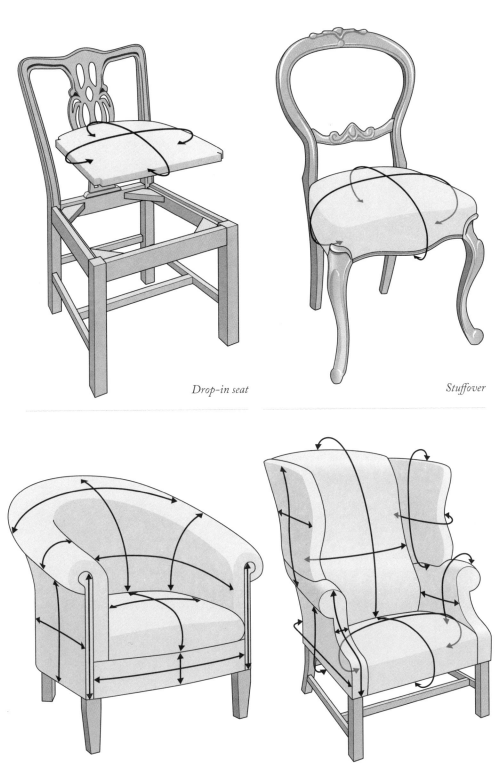

Drop-in seat

Stuffover

Tub chair

Wing chair

Detail of pattern distortion down a seam

The effect of using a vertical stripe.

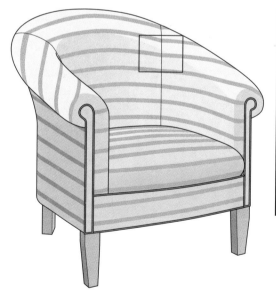

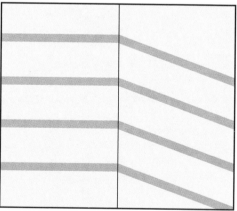

The effect of using a horizontal stripe.

Pattern repeats and pattern placement

The size of the pattern repeat will be given on the fabric label and it has a significant effect on the amount of fabric that you need for your upholstery project. With small pattern repeats such as a small check or plaid fabric, you will get many repeats of the pattern over a relatively small area such as a drop-in seat. With a large pattern repeat (27½" [70 cm] square, for example), you might not even be able to fit the entire pattern within the seat area. With a small pattern repeat there tends to be less waste because you can cut the fabric more economically (see Cutting Plans on page 79). When calculating how much fabric to buy, you must take the size of the pattern repeat into account. For beginners, it's generally best to stick to small patterns or plain fabrics.

Choosing which part of the pattern should be prominent on each panel is very subjective and can depend on the chair shape as much as on the upholsterer's personal taste. You may hear upholsterers talking about "corridors": these are focal points on a piece of furniture to which our eyes tend to be drawn. Rather then being something to be intimidated by, I tend to use these areas as a guide to where the pattern alignment should be at its most consistent.

Key focal points tend to be directly in the center of the chair, running up the front of the seat, from front to back across the center of the cushion, and up the back, up the front of the arm, along the top of the arms and along the leading edge of any wing.

Railroading

Occasionally you may come across a "railroaded" fabric. This is all to do with the orientation of the pattern. Usually fabric patterns run "up the roll," meaning that the pattern is woven from top to bottom, parallel with the selvedges. On a fabric that has been specifically woven as railroaded, the pattern runs across the roll from selvedge to selvedge.

The accepted convention in upholstery is generally that patterns should run from top to bottom and from back to front: stripes, for example, generally look best if they run vertically rather than horizontally. Most upholstery fabrics are 54" (140 cm) wide. On an "up the roll" pattern, this would mean that you'd have to stitch a seam every 54" (140 cm).

Using a railroaded fabric, where the stripes run across the width of the roll, means that the pattern can run over a much longer stretch—as long, in theory, as the roll of fabric.

If a fabric has been woven specifically as a railroaded fabric, this information will be given in the pattern book or fabric label.

Provided you're using a fabric with a non-directional pattern, you can effectively create a railroaded fabric from a conventional-width fabric yourself, simply by marking out the panel pieces along the length rather than across the width. Be aware, however, that this may change the way the light affects the fabric pattern or the nap (pile direction) on fabrics such as velvet.

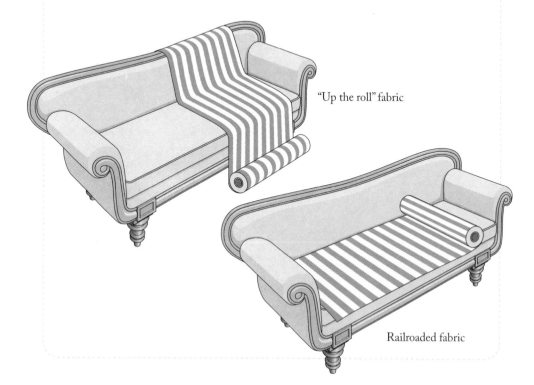

"Up the roll" fabric

Railroaded fabric

Making a cutting plan

Cutting plans are normally done to a scale of 1:10 (based on the width of the fabric). Most upholstery fabrics are 54" (140 cm) wide, so take a piece of paper and draw two parallel lines down it 5.4" (14 cm) apart. This represents the width of the fabric. Then make marks every 4" (10 cm) down these two parallel lines—these divide the fabric into 40" (1 meter) lengths so that, once you've drawn all the pieces on your cutting plan, you can work out how many yards you need to buy.

Now take all the individual measurements that you made earlier and transfer them to the cutting plan, remembering to align the warp direction up and down the roll and the weft from side to side. Also allow for seam allowances, turnings, and pattern repeats. (Being a natural pessimist, I always order extra fabric to allow for slight errors in measuring, things going wrong during the upholstery process or any inherent faults within the fabric itself!)

It can take several attempts to work out the most efficient and least wasteful layout. You may find it easier to draw each individual panel at a scale of 1:10 and physically lay them on your cutting plan. Then you can move them around easily and ensure that wastage is kept to a minimum. Even experienced upholsterers may find this a useful exercise when working with a very expensive fabric.

In an ideal world, you'd simply be able to scale your cutting plan back up to the size you need. However, inconsistencies in the weave of the fabric, creases that have formed while the fabric is on the roll, and general flaws in the weave mean that a cutting plan generally serves as a guide rather than a template. It's important to become familiar with cutting plans as a general principle, but don't get too entrenched in working out every single detail, such as where the main pattern element is to be positioned on each panel.

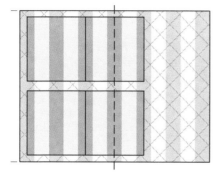

Wasteful cutting plan

Although this layout allows you to cut four dining-chair covers with the striped pattern in exactly the same place each time, the long strip on the right-hand side is too narrow to be of much use, so this fabric is likely to be wasted.

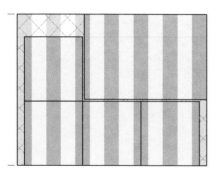

Economical cutting plan

By butting the panels up against each other, again cutting through the center of the dark stripes each time, you create an offcut large enough to cover another two chairs.

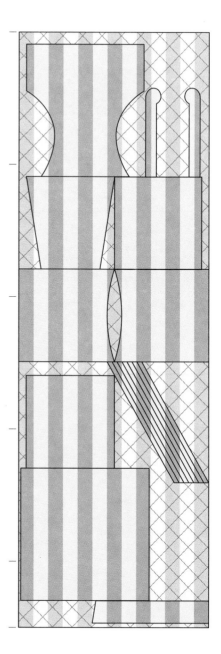

Tub-chair cutting plan for striped fabric

Because the pattern is easy to match from one panel to the next, very little fabric is wasted: this cutting plan only requires just under 5 yards (4.5 meters) of fabric.

Cutting plan for drop-in pads with large motif
Like the striped dining-chair covers on the opposite page, each panel is identical—but with a big, bold fabric pattern, as here, where the large rose motif needs to sit in the center of each pad, you cannot butt the pieces up against each other so there is always going to be more wastage.

Tub-chair cutting plan for large-patterned fabric
The pieces are exactly the same as on the striped fabric wing-chair cutting plan opposite—but the need to have the rose motif in the center of each "corridor" means that more fabric is required—here 6 yards (5.5 meters).

Warp and weft

The warp threads are the strands of thread that are threaded vertically onto the loom; the weft threads come from the shuttle that passes through the warp threads from side to side. (A simple rhyming way to remember which is which is, "weft has a left!")

Marking out your fabric panels

It's unlikely that you'll be able to mark everything up in advance, as you'll be limited by the length of your cutting table. Select the panels that you'll be upholstering first—typically, either the arms or the back—and mark them out with tailor's chalk on the reverse side of the fabric, making sure that you label the top edge or front edge of each piece as you go, as well as identifying which panel you're dealing with.

Ensuring pattern alignment and continuity on the finished panel is best dealt with at the cutting table. First, identify each "corridor" and which part of the pattern is going to be prominent through that corridor; then make sure that the center of each panel that you mark aligns with the center of the pattern on the roll of fabric. I find it helps to cut a small notch at the center of the top and bottom edges of each panel as I go. When I come to apply the fabric, I can then match these notches with marks made on the frame of the piece and be confident that everything is in the right place.

Professional tips

☐ All marking should be done on the reverse side of the fabric.

☐ With a delicate fabric or fabric that has a pile, take care to mark lightly—pressing hard with the chalk may well emboss lines on the front of the fabric.

☐ Maintain a sharp edge on the chalk so that you keep the line thin. If the chalk is blunt, it can make a thick line and it can be confusing to know which side of the line to cut. Sharpening can be done with a knife or a specialist chalk-sharpening tool.

☐ I always try to choose a chalk color as close as possible to the fabric color to avoid smudging dye from the chalk onto the fabric.

☐ If you make a mistake when marking out, removing the chalk can be difficult because of the wax. Trying to rub the chalk out is likely to be the least successful option; instead, try a blast of compressed air (if available) or a solvent-based cleaning solution in a well-ventilated space.

Cutting fabric

You don't need to cut everything out as soon as you've marked the panels on the roll of fabric—you can leave the panels on the roll until you're ready to use them. Storing lots of awkwardly shaped pieces can be tricky, but keeping them on the roll means there is less risk of creasing—an important consideration if you're working with a fabric such as velvet.

It's absolutely critical to have sharp shears to get a clean cut and reduce strain on your cutting hand. I have one pair that I use only for cutting single layers of fabric. (For multiple layers, I use electric cutters.) Use the full length of blade wherever possible, as this will reduce both the number of times you have to open and close the shears and the risk of getting a jagged-edged cut. Some fabrics such as damasks and brocades have details woven into them that will be slightly tougher to cut through than the fabric around the motif; this is where any unsharpened parts of the shears may snag.

As soon as you've cut out the panel, chalk mark the appropriate edge of the reverse with a letter "T" (for top) or "F" (for front) and label it with the panel name (or an abbreviation) so that you don't mix them up or get them the wrong way round.

Professional tip

If you're not putting the panels on the piece of furniture immediately, hang them over something like a towel rail, a curtain pole or the rounded back of a chair so that they don't get creased. (In the workshop, we use a kind of improvised A-frame clothes horse, made from plywood, with rounded rails to drape the fabric over.)

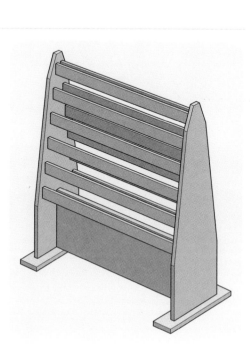

Ripping down

Ripping down (also known as "stripping out") simply means removing existing fabric and fillings. It may (but does not always) involve taking the piece back to the bare frame.

First, select a table or workbench that is at the right height. Stand up, with your arms straight by your sides: the ideal table height for ripping down would be roughly around where your wrist is, as this allows you to work without having to stoop. Second, make sure that the table is sturdy and will not wobble around while you are working.

Put a protective cloth, old sheet or blanket on your workbench to catch any debris. The cloth will also help to absorb some of the impact of using the mallet. If possible, clamp the item of furniture to the workbench using a speed cramp.

It's worth wearing a dust mask, plus protective goggles to stop any splinters from flying up into your eyes; I advise my students to use safety spectacles rather than traditional goggles, as they are less likely to steam up when used in conjunction with a dust mask. Ear plugs dull the repetitive sound of banging the mallet against the tool in hand. It's also a good idea to keep a vacuum cleaner at hand, so that you can clean up the dust as you remove each successive layer. This not only removes potentially harmful dust, but also makes it easier for you to assess the condition of the frame and fillings.

Your first step is to remove the bottom cloth or dust cover and see what's underneath.

Professional tip

It's a good idea to take photos as you go, to remind yourself of the different layers in the original piece. (These are also great to have as "before and after" shots so that, at the end of the process, you can see the transformation you've brought about!)

Removing tacks

To remove the tacks, you will need a ripping chisel or tack lifter and a mallet. The idea is to lift the tack slightly with the first strike of the ripping chisel, and then knock it out completely with as few blows as possible.

If chair legs or decorative wood inhibit the angle at which you can approach the first tack, start about one-third of the way along the rail, with the chisel pointing in the same direction as the grain of the wood, as this offers the least resistance. Work your way along to the end of the rail from right to left, then come back and knock out the remaining tacks from left to right, with the chisel at 180 degrees to its original position.

The number of times you need to hit the chisel into the tack will vary depending on a combination of factors:

☐ The size and shape of the tack.

☐ The type of wood, and the tightness and direction of the wood grain.

☐ The moisture content of the wood; this generally reduces with age and effectively tightens the wood grain.

☐ The thickness and condition of the rail holding the tack.

☐ Proximity to polished wood.

☐ The thickness of the material being removed.

☐ The number of layers that are being held by each tack.

☐ The condition of the tacks that you are lifting.

Removing tacks with a tack lifter

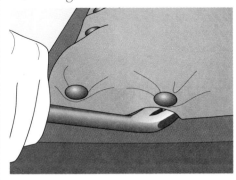

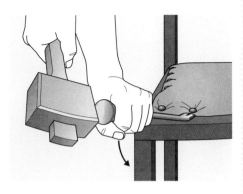

1 Align the center of the prongs with the shaft of the tack.

2 Strike the end of the tack lifter with the mallet, in the same way as with the ripping chisel (see page 86), then rock the handle of the tack lifter downward to lift up the tack.

Removing tacks with a ripping chisel

1 Holding the ripping chisel firmly at a low angle to the rail, butt the tip up against the head of the tack, being careful not to gouge into the wood of the frame. Hold the mallet with your little finger level with the end of the mallet handle; this allows you to swing the mallet with minimum effort and maximum force.

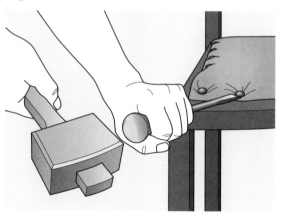

2 Strike the end of the chisel firmly with the mallet. This should prise up the tack head, although you may not drive it out at the very first attempt.

3 For difficult tacks, slip the chisel head under the fabric pointing up toward the tack, then proceed as above.

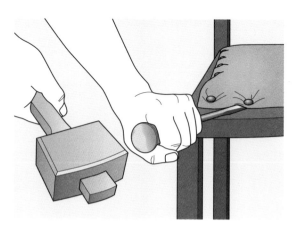

Removing staples

To remove staples, you will need a mallet, a staple lifter, pincers, and/or side cutters. Different staple removers work in slightly different ways, but the basic principle is the same—to lever the staple up far enough for you to be able to grip it with pincers or pliers and then pull it out. To speed up the process, you can loosen a whole row of staples with the remover, then pick up the pincers to complete the removal process.

Overshooting the staple or slipping out from under the staple and stabbing the end of the staple remover into a beautifully polished rail is a trauma apprentice and master upholsterers know all too well. It can and will happen: it's simply a reality of ripping down.

Stage 1: Loosening the staple

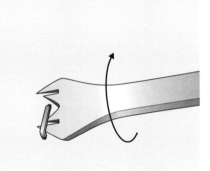 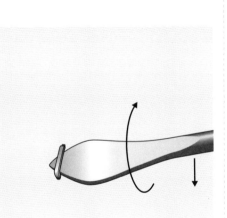

1a First, position the staple remover under the wire of the staple. With Osborne and Berry staple lifters, hook one prong of the tool under the staple wire, then simply apply vertical force (Osborne) or rotate your wrist (Berry) to lever up the staple.

1b With the spade-type remover, hook the point of the spade under the center of the wire, then lever both prongs of the staple out. With all these tools, if you can't slip the tip under the staple wire, position the tool and then gently tap the handle with a mallet.

Whichever tool you choose, there should be enough of the staple wire visible for you to use carpenter's pincers or pliers to pull it out completely. Start off slowly until you get a feel for the tension you need to use to lift the staple without snapping it.

Stage 2: Pulling the staple out

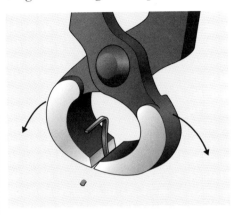

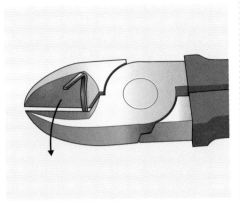

2a To use carpenter's pincers, grip the staple where it is poking out of the wood as lightly as you can without the pincers slipping, then rock the head of the pincers backward or forward and slowly lift out the staple.

2b With side cutters, twist the handle of the cutters anticlockwise to lever the staple out.

Knowing when to give up!

If stubborn fragments of staples or tacks simply refuse to budge, it's often better to concede defeat than to carry on and cause excessive damage to the wood or board material. You win no prizes for removing every part of every fixing. Provided the bulk of the fixings are removed, the few that remain will not prevent the new fixings from gripping into your wood.

Instead of doggedly continuing, use a smaller-headed hammer (such as an upholsterer's hammer) to tap in any bits of metal poking out from the rail. Ensuring that there are no jagged spikes protruding from the frame will stop you from scratching or cutting your fingers as you progress through the project. And if you're working in a larger workshop, it is a matter of courtesy to ensure that the frame is "clean" and free of broken staples or tacks if someone else is going to work on the piece.

Basic frame repair

Once you've removed all the original upholstery, you can assess what repairs need to be done to the frame. I prefer to make all the joints stable first, before treating and cleaning the frame.

It is worth noting that frames settle with time to fit the floor that they are supported by, so if you're upholstering an antique chair, you may wish to inquire if it will be returning to the same spot. I have had customers who prefer a chair not to be made square during re-upholstering.

Re-gluing joints

It's beyond the scope of this book to go into huge detail about how to replace joints. If the piece you're working on requires this level of repair, it's generally best to take it to a specialist restorer, as I do. However, re-gluing joints that have worked loose is relatively simple, provided the elements that make up the joint are intact. Start by lightly tapping the inside edges of the rails: any joints that are loose or broken will open up slightly so you can take a peek. By using a vacuum cleaner to suck out dust or blowing away the dust from around the joint with compressed air, you should be able to see between the wooden rails and determine whether it is just loose or indeed broken. If you then shine a torch through the gap, it will be easier for you to see what kind of joint you're dealing with and whether you just need to carry out a simple repair or do something more complicated.

Once you have identified which joints are accessible, the next stage is to prise them apart carefully one at a time. You can do this using either a mallet or a spreader bar. The ideal gap to have is ¼–⅜" (5–10 mm). Any less than this and the gap will be too narrow to get sufficient glue into the joint; any more, and you are in danger of opening it too far.

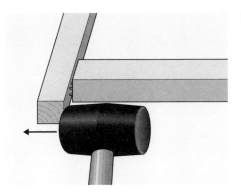

1a Rather than levering the joints apart with a chisel or staple remover, which will damage the wood around the joint, tap the rails lightly with a mallet to spread them apart.

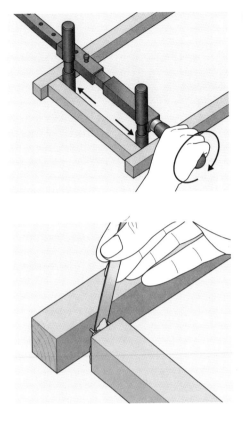

1b Alternatively, insert a reversible sash cramp between the rails, then turn the handle to push them apart in a controlled way.

2 To get the glue into the joint, I use either a thin strip of cardboard such as a back-tacking strip (see page 211) or a wooden coffee stirrer from a fast-food outlet, rather than pouring the glue directly onto the piece of furniture. Just put a blob of your chosen glue onto the applicator, then place it where you want it to go and scrape it along the joint. You'll need to do this two or three times to build up the required amount of glue and ensure that you've worked the glue evenly in and around all components of the joint.

3 To close up the joint, either lightly tap the wood with a mallet or reverse the heads on the sash cramp to the clamping position and allow the glue plenty of time to set. When it's tight enough, a small amount of glue will ooze out (provided you've applied glue in the first place!). Depending on the type of glue you've selected, this may be the right time to wipe off any excess.

4 To prevent any glue that has seeped out of the joint from adhering to polished wood and spoiling the finish, rub beeswax around the outside of the joint before you glue it.

Wood glues

PVA glues are the most common and most readily available type of wood glue. Once it has set, the glue will flex to a slight degree, allowing the joint to stress a little with use without breaking. It is easy to clean up any excess glue spilling out the joint as it's tightened in the cramp by wiping it away with a dampened cloth.

Thixotropic expanding wood glue is manufactured by several companies, and is available through more specialist suppliers. It does not flex in the same way as PVA, so it can become brittle in a chair frame that does a lot of flexing. Where it has an advantage over PVA is that it expands to fill small gaps, compensating for any wood that has worn away. Wiping up any excess glue can be a little tricky, so it's best to allow it to harden and then pick the excess off in lumps.

Of these two glues, PVA is the easier to work with if you are just starting out, but more experienced upholsterers should give the thixotropic glue a try, as it can be sourced in a 30-minute and a 5-minute cure versions, which is very handy if you are executing a last-minute re-glue or adding corner blocks and can't afford the time that PVA would take to grip.

If you are undertaking the conservation of an antique chair or are looking for a natural product, then traditional glues made from bones are still available widely through specialist suppliers.

Treating for woodworm

If you discover evidence of woodworm, don't panic—it may be centuries old. An easy way of working out if the woodworm is live is to tap the suspected rail lightly with a hammer and look for frass—a very fine, powdery, sawdust-like material, which will shower down from the rail onto your work surface. If no frass comes out, then you're probably dealing with old woodworm.

If the woodworm is live, apply a proprietary woodworm treatment—readily available from DIY stores. If you're in any doubt, apply a woodworm treatment anyway.

Filling old tack holes

Instead of using wood filler, which tends to be fairly hard and inflexible, a very simple and cost-effective option is to mix PVA glue with fine sawdust and make a thick paste. Carefully apply this to the rail and spread a thin layer along it, as if you're icing a cake. Leave to set, preferably for around 24 hours, then sand it level using a medium-to-fine grit sandpaper. Remember, though, that the more you put on, the more you'll have to sand off. I advise sanding by hand, rather than using an electric sander, so that, if you slip with the tool or sand too much, you won't damage the show wood around the rails.

Marking the frame

At this stage, adding some marks to the frame will make later stages much easier as you'll have a guideline to ensure that you place your tacks the same distance apart and that your stitches are similar in length.

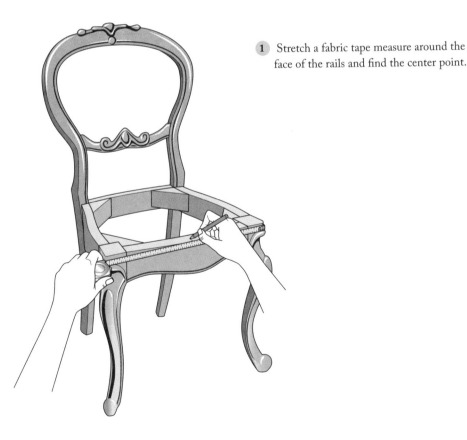

1 Stretch a fabric tape measure around the face of the rails and find the center point.

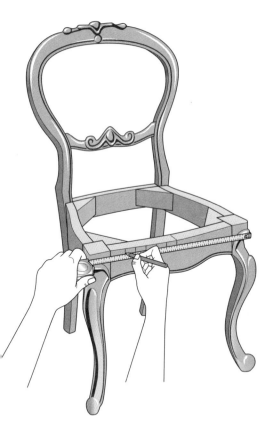

2 Starting from the center point, make a series of marks 1" (2.5 cm) apart on the front face of the rails, using either pen or pencil. (You can use chalk, but it may well wear off as you work through the different processes, so will need to be re-applied before you create the edge stitches—see page 169).

3 Your marks should be long and thick enough to see clearly, but take care not to mark the show wood.

Suspension systems

CHAPTER 3
Suspension systems

Building a firm yet flexible foundation for the padding is the initial stage in constructing most upholstered pads. Suspension systems have tended to follow two key directions: webbing and springing. Each loads stresses into the frame in different ways and not all webbing or springing types are suitable for all frames.

In most cases, particularly if you're a beginner, you'll be replacing an existing suspension system, like for like, so the decision on which suspension system to use has already been made for you.

Basic knots

Most processes require stitches to bind them together to form a cohesive system and these processes usually start with a knot of some kind. These knots are not particularly unusual, although there are, of course, idiosyncrasies that make them relevant to upholstery. With a little practice you should be able to pick them up fairly quickly.

Upholsterer's slip knot

An upholsterer's slip knot is used to fasten on twine or cord when starting to stitch and is the initial knot in a variety of upholstery processes, such as tying down a spring (see page 115).

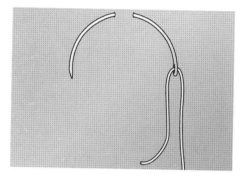

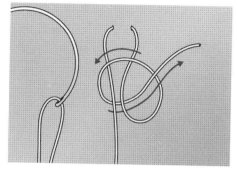

1 Thread a curved needle with a length of twine no longer than the span of your two arms outstretched. Insert the needle into the fabric from the front, take it all the way through, then bring it up again about ½" (1 cm) further along, leaving a tail of twine about 3" (7.5 cm) long.

2 Hold the two strands of twine parallel to one another. Take the short end of the twine over the two strands, so that you form a loop, then bring the short end up through the loop.

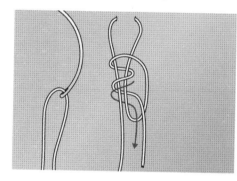

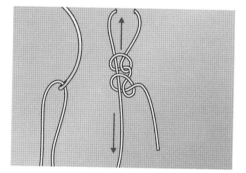

3 Repeat step 2.

4 Pull the loops taut and push them up the twine with your thumb, so that they sit against the fabric. This will hold the twine securely in place.

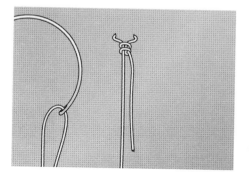

5 A completed double slip knot.

Half-hitch knot

A half-hitch knot is the most basic knot in upholstery and tightens slightly under tension. You will need a springing needle or a 6" (15-cm) curved needle. Half-hitches are used in upholstery to tie off (bind off) the ends of rows of stitches to pull materials together—for example, as part of a bridle tie (see page 163) or, as here, to hold springs to the underside of the webbing. They are also used in bridle ties to secure springs to burlap (see page 141) and to tie off (bind off) the ends of rows of stitches (see page 173).

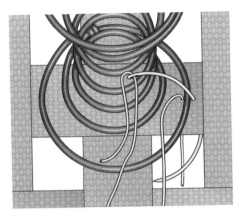

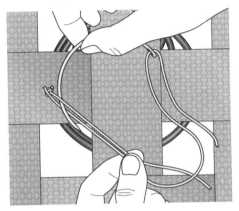

1 Secure the spring on the webbing with a slip knot (see page 93). From the underside of the webbing, insert the needle into the webbing on the inside of the spring coil, as close to the wire as possible. Draw the thread through so that it's taut. Take the needle over the spring wire and take it back down through the webbing, again keeping as close to the wire as possible to prevent the spring from slipping around.

2 With your non-working hand, hold the twine taut about 3" (7.5 cm) from the point where it emerges on the underside of the webbing, keeping it in line with the twine between the slip knot and the point where you're making the half-hitch.

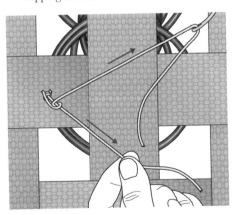

3 Take the needle under the twine that's come from the slip knot and over the twine that you're holding and pull tight.

Clove hitch knot

A clove hitch knot is the principal knot used to lash springs to one another to form one coherent unit to make them work together. The main advantage of a clove hitch knot is that it actually tightens itself around the spring wire as tension is applied.

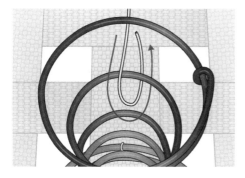

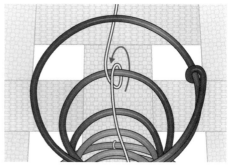

1 As a general rule, cut a length of cord roughly 1.5 times the length of the span between the rails. Lay the cord over the second coil of the spring wire.

2 Bring the far end back around under the wire to form a loop, then cross the loose tail of cord over the top to form an X-shape.

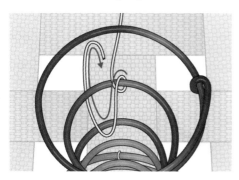

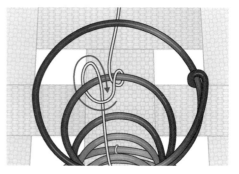

3 Bring the cord back around below the wire, forming a loose loop.

4 Feed the cord tail through the loop and pull to tighten. At this stage, it will look like a figure eight.

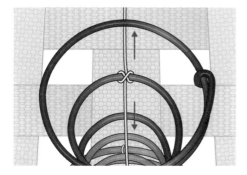

5 This figure-eight shape will squeeze up as the knot is tightened and will end up as a tight cross shape on the top of the wire.

Webbing

Let's start by looking at webbing, as this is both the simplest method for complete beginners to master and the one that lies at the heart of most modern upholstery.

Natural-fiber webbings either support springs or (with the addition of burlap) provide a base for fillings. If you're upholstering a pad with a natural filling such as horsehair or coir, it's generally best to go for a natural-fiber webbing; the webbing itself does not flex, so by using a loose filling you can control both the shape and density of the pad at the next stage. A non-flexible filling such as foam would take the whole of the load placed on the pad and consequently degrade more quickly.

Rubber and elasticated webbings do flex and they are more suited to providing a base for pre-fabricated fillings such as foam. The webbing and filling share the load placed on the pad, so the whole system is likely to last for longer.

When fixed onto a frame and interwoven to form a lattice, natural-fiber webbings distribute pressure evenly around the frame edges. Rubber and elasticated webbings are more typically fitted in just one direction, running up and down on a back or arm or from front to back on a seat.

Spacing the webs

Estimating the correct spacing for webs is partly a matter of personal choice and partly down to the choice of fiber and weaving techniques in different countries. (Traditional black-and-white webbing used in the United Kingdom, for example, is woven in a herringbone pattern, which gives it greater inherent strength than some other webbings.)

Traditional British and European furniture tends to have more space between the webs than North American furniture, and I was taught to space webs up to a hand's width apart. While working in Canada where 2½" (6-cm) 100% jute webbing was commonly used, however, I began to notice that high-quality 1970s and 1980s furniture that was being re-upholstered did not need the webbing replaced; even after 30 years of use, the fibers were strong enough to cope with a quick tightening. The key feature of these webbed seats was not that they used wider webbing, but the webbing was fitted with no spaces in between. Since then, I tend to aim for a two-finger spacing between my webs, which creates a significantly tighter lattice than I was taught was acceptable. I do not butt them together completely, because I need to be able to feed a needle through the web and reach through the gaps with my fingertips to draw the needle through. Another advantage of this is that you can run your fingers along the gap between webs and feel whether or not the spacing is consistent.

The two-finger spacing method is by no means the only valid method. If your budget will allow it, it's acceptable to place the webs with no spaces between them; one drawback is that if you intend to stitch springs to the webs, it will be harder to work from underneath when passing the needle through. And on antique furniture where the rail is already weak, you may end up overloading it with tacks and structurally weakening it.

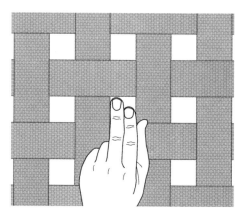

An alternative method that works well in conjunction with larger coil springs is to put two webs close together where the spring will be positioned and to have a gap between the pairs.

SPACING WEBS IN PAIRS
Larger springs require tighter webbing. Spacing the webs in pairs, with a two-finger space between the pairs, works well.

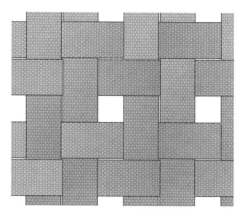

It is worth noting at this juncture that webbing intended to provide the suspension without the addition of springs is usually fixed to the top or the front of a rail, while webbing that is intended to have springs attached to it is usually fitted to the underside or the outside of a rail. The principal reason for attaching webbing to either the underside or the outside of a rail is that, if the webbing needs be serviced (tightened) or replaced with new, it can be done with the minimum of fuss.

Positioning the webs

Ensuring that webs run parallel to each other or taper evenly is more than just professional pride in the crafting of an upholstered pad—for me, it is a vital part of the process of familiarizing myself with the shape of the frame. Marking the frame with tailor's chalk will take the guesswork out of this and help you to get a pleasing finish.

When positioning the webs, you have to take the shape of the frame into account. Not all pads are square or rectangular, so you can't always place the webs in a precise grid formation, evenly spaced and at 90 degrees to each other. If the seat pad is narrower at the back than at the front, for example, or if the center front of the seat juts out, you will have to taper the angle of the webs accordingly. If part of the pad is going to be under the inside back or an arm when the piece is finished, then you don't need to run a cross-layer of webs directly under this area as they will not provide additional support.

If the piece of furniture is symmetrical, make sure that your web placement is symmetrical and even. If it is shaped, try to ensure that the webs are positioned to reflect this shape, using the two-finger spacing method as a guide as far as possible.

Start by fitting all the webs running in one direction first—for example, from front to back—and then interweave webs running in the opposite direction (from side to side). It doesn't really matter which way round you work, but as a general rule I start with the shortest lengths.

With all webbed panels, I start with the outer webs first. Every time you add a web to a frame, it becomes easier to get the correct tension on the next web, as the first web is already taking part of the strain. Because wooden rails can flex a little, it's often the case that if you put the center web in first it slackens slightly each time you put in a web to one side of it. This effect is noticeably reduced if you start from the outside edges and work in toward the center.

Marking the frame

1 If you haven't already done so (see page 92), chalk a line all around the edge of the frame at least ⅜" (1 cm) in from the outer edge of the rail. Not tacking beyond this line will help to prevent the folded edge of the web from interfering with the edge of the frame shape.

2 Now mark where all the webs will go. Work out how many webs you need by dividing up the space evenly. When you've worked out the spacing, mark where the center of each web will go, as the center tack is easiest to align.

Attaching woven natural-fiber webbing

1 Fold the raw end of the webbing to get a straight edge. Place the fold on your previously chalked line. Don't be tempted to guess how much webbing you will need and cut it to length at this stage: leave the webbing on the roll until you've tacked down the second end.

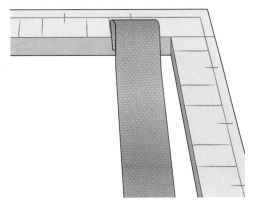

2 Aligning the tack with the mark you chalked to show the center of the web, tack or staple the webbing to one rail. Insert the center tack first, then one on either side of it, then two tacks in the spaces below, so that you end up with five tacks in a "W" formation.

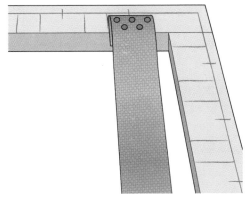

3 Now feed the webbing into your chosen stretcher: the way you do this depends on the type of stretcher you are using (see pages 107–109).

4 Pull the webbing across to the second rail and find the appropriate tension for that style of stretcher and webbing.

5 Insert three tacks in a row, as in step 2, then cut the webbing off the roll, leaving at least 2" (5 cm) beyond the tacks.

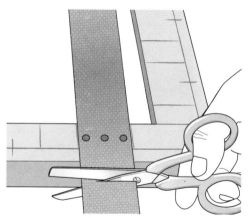

6 Fold the webbing back over the tacks, then insert two more tacks through both layers of webbing, so that you now have five tacks in the same "W" formation as at the other end of the webbing.

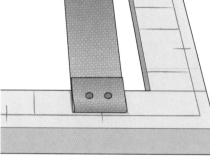

7 If you're using staples instead of tacks, stagger their positions so that you get a formation like bricks in the wall.

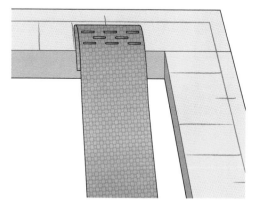

Feeding the webbing into the stretcher

After you've attached the first end of the webbing to the rail, you need to feed it into the stretcher.

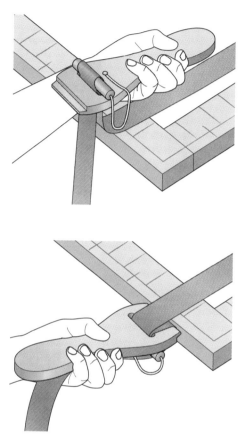

Slot-and-peg web stretcher

1 Hold the stretcher with the wider end toward your body and the handle farthest away; I prefer to have the notch facing upward at this stage. Thread the webbing through the slot, forming a loop above the stretcher, and pass the dowel peg through the loop.

2 Pull the webbing so that it closes moderately tightly around the peg and adjust the overall length of the web so that your stretcher overhangs the frame a little.

3 Now press the wider end of the stretcher against the frame and pull the tip of the handle over and toward you, making sure that you have trapped the webbing against the frame to prevent it from slackening. I like to hold the loose end of the webbing close to the handle to prevent it from getting tangled or rucking and possibly bruising the wood.

Latch stretcher

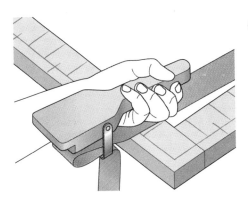

1 Hold the latch stretcher with the wide body closest to you and the slim end farthest away. The difference between this and the slot-and-peg stretcher is that the latch is underneath the tool, closest to the web. Push the loop of webbing through the latch mechanism and close it, allowing the excess webbing to hang down, and then adjust the length of strap to suit the distance required.

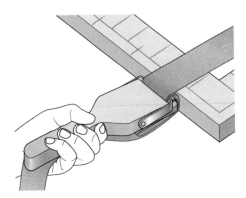

2 To use the stretcher, turn it upside down so that the latch side is uppermost, press the wide end against the frame and pull the handle downward to tension the webbing.

3 Once the webbing is attached to the second side of the frame, a simple flick of the tool will release it and you are free to cut and close the end of the web. It will save what may feel like a tiny amount of time on just one web, but if you are applying dozens those few moments saved can add up to a substantial time saving. This particular style of latch stretcher is limited to webbing 2" (5 cm) wide, but I have seen several home-made versions suited to wider webbings and made with differing styles of latch mechanisms.

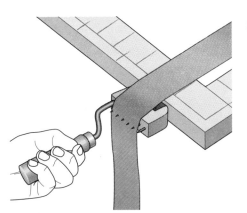

Goose- or swan-neck stretcher

1 Place the rubber grip located on the head of the tool against the outside edge of the second rail, so that the spikes are pointing upward. Hook the webbing onto the spikes, ensuring that the webbing is moderately taut but not overstretched. Brace the rubber end of the webbing stretcher against the outside of the furniture frame and apply pressure to the handle in a downward motion, which will tighten the webbing.

The correct tension for webbing

How tight should the webbing be? Getting a feel for the correct tension is something that you will learn with experience, but plucking the side of the webbing as though it were the string of a musical instrument should give you some guidance. Regardless of the distance that you are spanning, the webbing should resonate with an audible tone. Dull thuds and strangled twanging sounds give you the two ends of the spectrum, so aim for something in between. Do not overtighten the webbing or you may distort the shape of the frame. Allow the webs to bear the load evenly, without overstressing the rails or breaking any joints. Once you have found the correct tension, hold the stretcher in a comfortable position with your non-hammering hand or use a knee or hip to stabilize the stretcher, ready for tacking or stapling off.

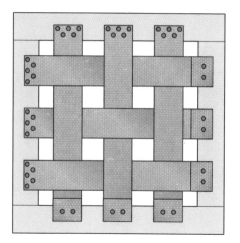

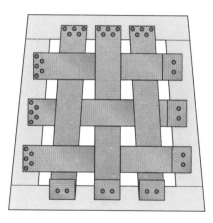

SYMMETRICAL PAD

On a symmetrical pad, the webs, too, should be positioned symmetrically. For a relatively small, square dining-chair pad, a "grid" of three webs from front to back and three from side to side, all evenly spaced, will normally suffice.

TAPERED PAD

Here, the webs taper inwards slightly to match the tapered shape of the pad. Again, a 3 x 3 grid provides sufficient support.

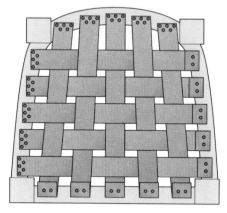

SERPENTINE EDGE

The front of the seat requires plenty of support, so the webs in this area slant inwards from the center of the seat to the sides, echoing the shape of the front rail. Behind the shaped front edge, the webs are spaced evenly.

AREAS UNDER THE INSIDE BACK AND INSIDE ARM

The area under the inside back and inside arm is not sat on, so space is left at the back.

Rubber webbing as used by Ercol furniture.

Attaching rubber webbing

Rubber webbing is often exposed under a seat cushion and is designed to grip cushions to prevent them from sliding off the seat while it is in use. There is no reason why rubber webbing cannot be used within a pad, but it is considerably more expensive than elastic webbing.

Rubber webbing is generally fixed onto the frame with one of a variety of removable fixing clips, which fit into slots or rebates cut into the seat frame, although it can be stapled in place. With rubber webbing, understanding stretch isn't as obvious as it is with other springing systems and often boils down to striking a balance between the ideal tension and what it is physically possible to achieve. It's virtually impossible to gauge how much any old webs that you remove from a frame will have stretched with use, so to work out how much webbing you need it's vital to take accurate measurements from the frame, work out the size of the gap the webs need to span, make allowances for the frame and assess how much webbing the fixing uses.

Fitting rubber webbing with clips is very easy if you have a bench-mounted vice. If that's not an option, the clips can be crimped with pincers and tapped with a hammer to close them tight, but it is difficult to get the pressure even. Most upholstery workshops and online suppliers will cut the straps and fit the clips onto the ends for you relatively inexpensively, and if you only need a few I would advise getting them made up.

It is important to note that the flexibility of rubber products depends on the ambient temperature: fitting rubber straps in winter in a poorly heated workshop could lead to excessive slackening of the straps in the height of summer when they warm up and slacken off.

As with natural-fiber webbing, a two-finger spacing between webs is generally sufficient.

Professional tip

Different clip types have their own idiosyncrasies, but my top trick for fitting rubber webbing is to soak the straps in hand-warm water for 10 minutes prior to fitting, while ensuring that metal clip components don't get wet. Softening the rubber makes it stretch easily without straining the fibers inside. It should only take a few seconds to fit the straps and within a couple of minutes the webs will have cooled off and represent the correct tension.

Method

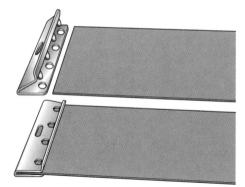

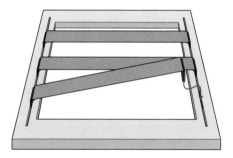

1 Fit a fixing clip to the end of the roll of rubber webbing.

2 Attach the clip to the first slot in the frame and stretch it tight across the frame. Without letting go, mark the webbing with a soft pencil at the point where the open end of the strap crosses the second slot. Adding this to the amount used by fitting the clip gives you the length of webbing you need for the strap. I make one up and try it in several places on the seat to make sure it fits all positions and then proceed with making the batch.

Professional tip

Sometimes, I'm asked to cut straps of rubber webbing to size without actually having the chair available for fitting. The following method is excellent for gauging the length while accommodating for the stretch.

1 Ask your client to measure from one slot in the frame to the other.

2 Take a piece of hardwood approximately 25" (65 cm) long, 4–6" (10–15 cm) wide and over 1" (2.5 cm) thick. Make a mark 2" (5 cm) in from one end, then cut a slot in the wood no deeper than ⅝" (1.5 cm). To get a slot ¼" (6 mm) wide, make a second parallel cut using a fine saw blade. Once you have cut the slot, clean it out by using a medium-grit piece of sandpaper to sand the inside edges a little.

3 Using a G-clamp, clamp the board to the workbench, fixing it halfway behind the slot and the short end. Using a yardstick, measure from the slot and mark across the board with a pencil: the distance between the slot and the marked line should be the same as the measurements you were given by your client.

Elasticated webbing

Elasticated webbing can be used for all the applications that rubber webbing can be used for, because 30% elasticity webbing performs in a very similar way to rubber webbing. It is fitted in the same way, using either clips or staples. It does have some drawbacks, however, as it doesn't grip cushions in the same way as rubber webbing, nor are the folded ends as strong. I tend to prefer rubber webbing to elasticated, because it blends into a wooden frame very smartly, which is most important when the webs can be seen, and it tends to last longer.

Assessing how much stretch elastic webbings require is becoming fairly easy, as they are increasingly being sold listing their stretch as a percentage. When fitting the webbing, stretch it beyond the slot in the rail by this percentage—this should give the correct tension while still allowing the webbing to flex a little during use. (For example, if the distance from one slot to the other is 39" (100 cm) and you're using a webbing with 30% elasticity, a strap length of 27½" (70 cm) should give the right tension.)

Most upholsterers typically carry a stock of three different strengths of elasticated webbing. Firmer seat webbings perform best around 30% elasticity. Softer seats can be achieved by using a web with either 60% or 70% elasticity, and 85–100% elasticity webbings are used almost exclusively for backs and give a much softer feel.

Combining a couple of types of elasticated webbing can give a greater scope of support for the sitter. For example, in the lumbar region of a chair back, two stronger webs running side to side at the correct height for that frame will give support in a similar fashion to springing.

Elasticated webbings will work perfectly well when spaced 2–3" (5–7.5 cm) apart for seats or chair backs. For inside armrests, a 4" (10-cm) spacing is more appropriate.

Covering webbing with burlap

When springs are not being used, it is normal to cover the webs with the heaviest weight of burlap available (see page 131). This layer of 12-oz (340-gram) burlap will not only help to displace the weight of the sitter evenly around the seat pad, but will also help to prevent the stuffing and batting from being forced out through the underside or back of the pad.

Individual springs

If springs are being used, they are fitted directly on top of the webbing, with no burlap in between.

Springs work in two very different ways. Coil or cone springs (see page 45) are usually attached on top of webbing and they compress to provide a flexible base for subsequent filling layers. Tension and serpentine springs (see pages 46–47) are fixed between two rails and they stretch to perform the same role. All springs add another level of comfort and support for the body; single-cone spring units (typically known as mesh-top units) and double-cone springs also fill space, thus adding volume to the pad. Mesh-top units are generally made to order to fit a particular frame and are simply slotted into place and secured with galvanized nails inserted through pre-drilled holes in the laths underneath the unit, so are easy to fix in place.

Tying double-cone springs to a webbed deck

Double-cone springs are tied over the intersections between either pairs of webs or a lattice of individual webs. Convention states that you should place a spring at each intersection, but if the webs are very closely spaced there may simply not be enough room for you to do this without the springs rubbing against each other and wearing through the lashings prematurely. Professional upholsterers may argue the merits of their own system, but as a guideline a spring spacing of around 2" (5 cm) between the coils should suit most applications.

The two diagrams above show good examples of springs placed on webbing in such a way as to obtain an even distribution of force.

You need to be able to see both the top and the underside of the webs to be sure you're attaching the springs in the right place, so work with the piece up on your workbench.

To tie the springs in place, I use a 6" (15-cm) curved bayonet-point needle when stitching the springs to a black-and-white webbing deck, as it allows the needle to cut through the tough herringbone weave. For jute webbing, a 6" (15-cm) round-point curved needle, which pushes the fibers out of the way, is adequate. I use nylon buttoning twine most of the time—partly because of its inherent strength, but also because it allows me to work just three half-hitch knots instead of four. When upholstering a large piece that can hold over 100 springs or more, eliminating one knot from every spring can add up to a substantial cost saving without compromising on quality. If you're using thick no. 6 linen twine, then a conventional springing needle may well be better suited, because the thicker blade and eye of the needle help the twine pull through the webbing without knotting and then snapping during stitching.

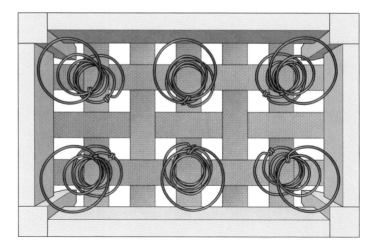

1 Start by placing the springs on the webbing so that you can plan where they will fit before you commit yourself to stitching them in place. If you are concerned that you may forget or lose track of where the springs are to be placed, simply draw around them on the webbing with chalk. Then you can remove them without fear of re-positioning them incorrectly.

2 Start by making a double slip knot (see page 97) to secure the first spring to the webbing by inserting the needle through the webbing from the underside. This can be a little difficult to get used to at first, as you are working blind, but it will get easier with practice.

Don't cut twine to more than the length of your two arms outstretched. The longer the twine, the more time you will have to spend pulling it through the webbing at each stage— don't underestimate how tiring this can be. And the longer the twine, the greater the risk of it getting tangled around a previously tied-in spring.

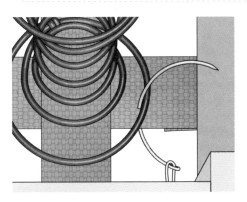

3 Hold the spring in place, keeping the mouth of the spring toward the outer edges of the frame with your non-working hand. With your other hand, push the threaded needle through the webbing from the underside so that it just touches the inside edge of the spring's bottom coil as it comes through. Draw the needle all the way through.

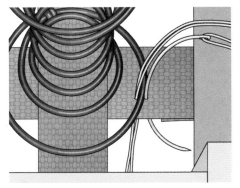

4 Take the needle over the bottom coil and push it back through the webbing, just touching the outside edge of the spring. It's important to make sure that you do not simply take the needle down through the same hole from which it emerged, as you need to gather some of the webbing and bind the spring to it with each knot.

5 Now tie the two ends of thread hanging down from the underside of the deck together using a double slip knot (see page 97), and draw the knot tight.

6. Now that the first spring is held loosely to the deck, rotate the spring to make sure that the mouth of the spring is facing an outer edge of the frame. This ensures that the knot of wire at the top of the spring will be less likely to cut through the burlap that is fitted to the top later on.

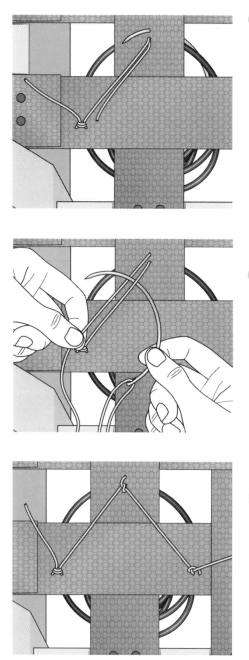

7. Imagine that the knot you have just made represents one point of an equilateral triangle: now put in the other two half-hitch knots (see page 98) at the remaining points of the triangle to hold the spring firmly to the deck. (With experience, you'll be able to do this by touch alone.) As with the first step of the slip knot, bring the needle up through the webbing, just touching the inside edge of the bottom coil of the spring. Take the needle over the wire to the outside of the spring and push it back down through the webbing.

8. Using your non-working hand, pull the twine all the way through so that it lays tight against the webbing, almost doubling back on itself. Hold the needle in your working hand and pass it under the length of twine that runs directly from the previous knot and over the looser length held in your non-working hand.

9. Simply pull the knot tight and you will have formed the easiest knot that can often cause the greatest of headaches. Repeat steps 7–9 at the third point in the triangle to secure the spring to the webbed deck.

Keep the distance to the first knot on the next spring to a minimum. There is no set pattern that will fit all seat, back or arm styles, but keeping the pattern that emerges as consistent as possible from one spring to the next will help to speed up the process.

Once all of the springs have been stitched to the webbing, repeat the last knot on the last spring several times to tie off (bind off) the stitches. Trim the excess twine, leaving a tail of no more than 2" (5 cm).

Some upholsterers might call for four knots to secure the underside of the spring to the web base, but I reserve this extra knot for when I am using no. 6 linen thread to tie the springs down, because the nylon twine that I normally use is so strong it doesn't require a fourth knot.

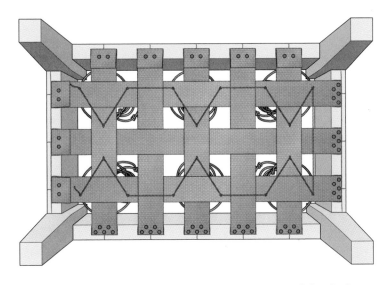

Here, all the springs have been tied down, using a single length of twine

Attaching serpentine springs

Serpentine springs do not need the thickness of pad that is associated with double-cone springs. The rails need to be in a good state of repair and it is advisable to use spring clips to attach the springs to the frame rather than fixing them directly onto the wood. This allows them to flex a little more and also prevents the metal from moving against the wood and squeaking.

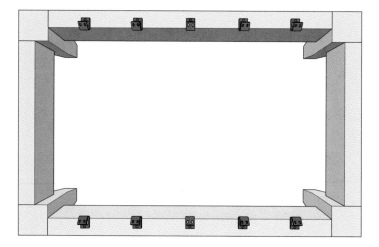

1 If you are going to simply replace the springs, then the clips will already be there. If you're working on a completely new piece, nail the first fixing clip in place on the front edge of the back rail, then fit the second clip directly in line with it onto the back edge of the front rail.

2 Assessing the length of spring to cut can be difficult for beginners so it's best to cut one, check the tension and use that as a pattern for cutting the remaining springs. Some serpentine springs come pre-cut in standard lengths and these offer the smartest solution when starting out: just select the length of spring that is just slightly shorter than the distance between the two rails. Similarly, if you are cutting the springs yourself from a roll, then cut a length just shorter than the span of your frame.

3 Hook the end loop of the spring into the first clip and tap the clip closed with a hammer.

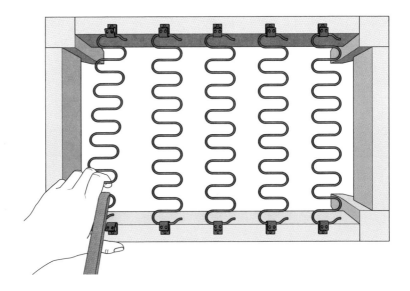

4 Stretch the spring across the gap and hook it onto the front-rail clip. The spring should be under a degree of tension, but it should feel easy to push the spring down.

With seat springs, if you have to pull them any more than 1" (2.5 cm) or so, then it is probably too short. If the spring is too long, unhook the front part of the spring and use bolt cutters (or a hack saw, although this is less precise) to cut one loop at a time off the spring, re-checking the tension every time until you have the tension required. This spring can then be used as a pattern from which to cut the others.

5 Once all of the springs are in place and the clips have been tapped closed, secure them shut with a second staple or nail, depending on the clip type.

Professional tip

Cutting guillotines and end loop benders are specialist pieces of kit and make the job much easier. They are the best solution for larger workshops; if you don't have them, bolt cutters will do the cutting well and bending the end returns can be done with the aid of a vice, a strong arm, and patience.

In the past, many companies used more elaborate webbing-type mountings, which typically had a simple cover sewn to the webbing that dressed over the springs and masked the hooked part of the spring at the point of attachment. These are becoming ever more difficult to source—and their inherent drawback is that the eyelets fixed to the webbing tend to pull out with use, causing the webbing to shred around the holes. Retired upholsterer Jimmy Johnson introduced me to this method which, with small changes, is the system I now use for attaching tension springs.

1. Start by measuring the depth of the seat from the back face of the front rail to the front face of the back rail and cut two pieces of straight 9-gauge spring wire that are approximately 2" (5 cm) shorter than this.

2. Now cut two lengths of jute or black-and-white webbing that are 2" (5 cm) longer than the wire. Turn the ends in by ¾" (2 cm) at either end and fold the webbing in half along its length. Ensuring that the ends are still tucked in, machine sew a line ⅜" (1 cm) in from the folded edge along the full length of the web. Once both webs are sewn, insert the wires between the fold and the stitching.

3. Cut two more lengths of webbing that are either long enough to tack onto the front and back rails or long enough for the ends to be hemmed. Sew one of the extra lengths to one of the first webs containing the wire, so that one side of the second web aligns with the unfolded edges of the first (wired) web. The flat second web should now overhang the folded webbing by at least ¾" (2 cm). It is this second web that will protect the cushion that will sit on the springs, so this web should be uppermost when fitted onto the chair.

4. Fix the unfolded edges of the webbing to the frame with either ½" (13-mm) fine tacks or staples.

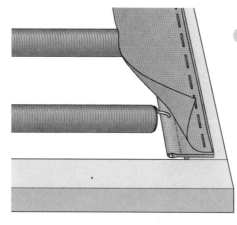

5. To fit the tension springs to the webbing, simply push the hooked end of the spring through the webbing, ensuring that the hooks go over the metal wire inside the webbing. Stretch the spring over to the opposite rail and attach in the same way.

Attaching tension springs

On the whole, it is easier to work out how long tension springs need to be: springs around 14–18" (35–45 cm) long work well with up to 1" (2.5 cm) of stretch; springs over this may need to be 1½" (4 cm) shorter than the span between the rails to give the correct tension when stretched and fitted.

The fixing plates most commonly available for tension springs are made from metal and have pre-drilled holes either side of the plate—one for fixing with nails to the frame and the other for clipping the springs into. Once you've worked out the spacing between the springs, nail the plates to the frame (making sure they align on opposite rails), then hook the springs onto the plates to secure them in place.

Lashing springs

Once the springs have been secured to the webbing deck and the panel or chair has been turned back upright, the springs need to be lashed both to each other and to the frame with laid cord. Lashing serves several purposes. It binds individual components together to make a cohesive unit and helps to spread the weight-bearing load over the springs. (For example, if you were to sit on one end of a couch, your weight might be directly over a handful of springs; because those springs have been lashed to the others in the frame, the load is distributed over all the springs, meaning that their life is increased.)

Lashing also stabilizes the springs so that they are only compressed downward and cannot shift from side to side. This makes the pad more comfortable and it also prevents uneven wear and tear on the filling levels above, again increasing the longevity of the upholstery.

With double-cone springs, lashing is an effective way of controlling the height of the spring, which enables the upholsterer to make either a very flat spring base or to build a rounded "crown."

Double-cone springs: four-way lashing

Springs may be either top lashed or center lashed. A top lash is, as you might expect, one that is tied from the frame to the top coil of the spring. A center lash is tied from the frame to the center, or "waist," of the spring.

Springs under 6" (15 cm) high can be lashed just across the top, whereas springs over this height generally need to be center lashed. (There are exceptions to the rule, of course: if the spring is for a back, then a center lash may not be required at this height, but in a seat it would be advisable.)

Whether you are tying a center lash or a top lash, the knot to use for holding the springs together is a clove hitch knot (see page 99). The advantage of a clove hitch knot is that it tightens around the spring when additional pressure is loaded into it.

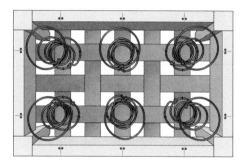

1 On opposite rails, in line with the springs, temporary tack (hammer in halfway) pairs of staples or robust tacks. (The size will depend on the width of the rail: for example, a ⅝" (16-mm) tack is ideal when being tacked into a thick seat rail, but would not suit a more slender dining seat rail where a ½" (13-mm) improved tack would be a better choice.)

2 Take a length of laid cord at least 1.5 times (but no more than twice) the distance between the rails. (You need a length that is long enough to lash the span of springs, but not one that is so long that it will get itself twisted around the springs.)

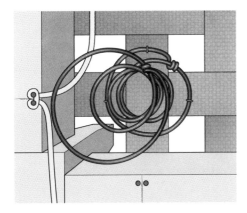

3 Measure twice the distance from the rail to the outer edge of the first spring, add 2" (5 cm) or so, and fold the cord that distance from the end to form a loop. Hook that loop over the two tacks so that the loop is on the inside edge of the rail. Feed the two ends in between the tacks and under the loop and draw tight. Leaving a long tail of laid cord either end of the lashing is essential: this extra cord will be used to apply a second reinforcing lash later in the process.

4 Hammer down the tacks. You now have a secure lark's foot fixing.

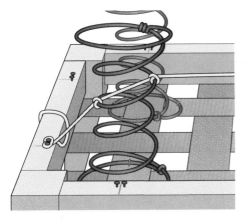

5 For a center lash, make a clove hitch knot halfway down the spring, at the waist. It is very important to ensure that the springs remain vertical, as this will limit unnecessary force from being applied to any one area of each spring as it flexes up and down during use. Then take the cord over level with your first clove hitch knot (see page 99).

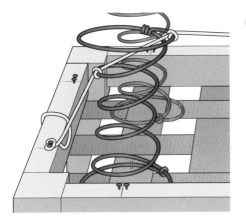

6 For a top lash, make a clove hitch knot on the lower loop of the mouth of the spring (the second coil), ensuring that the spring has not been bent over too much— otherwise when you finish lashing the whole area, you may find that the top loop of the spring is not directly above the base. Then take the cord up to the top loop of the same spring, moving away from the tacks on the rail, and form another clove hitch knot on that loop, directly opposite the first.

7 Continue laying the cord across the tops or centers of the row of springs and lashing them in the same way. For top lashes, make sure that the distance between the clove hitch knots on adjacent springs is the same as the distance between the bases of those two springs.

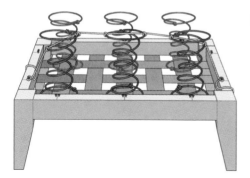

8 When you get to the last spring on the row, mirror what you did on the first one—on a row of top lashes, your last clove hitch knot will be on the second loop of the last spring. Pull the tension into the cord and then tie off (bind off) the cord around the tacks with a lark's foot fixing, feeding one end of the cord around the tacks and leaving a loose end of cord—this should be roughly the same length as the loose cord at the other end.

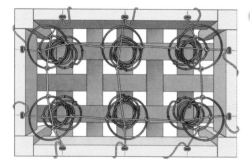

9 Repeat these steps, lashing the springs from front to back across the seat, and then again from side to side. This is known as four-way lashing and is the foundation of most spring-lashing techniques.

Professional tip

I find that students frequently tend to overtighten the span between the tacks and the first knot in a run, so I encourage loosely tacking one end or tying it round a temporary tack and then revisiting it later on once the lashes are all tied to tighten up or slacken off each end as required.

Eight-way lashing
This is an extension of four-way lashing and involves lashing the springs diagonally in both directions, as well as from front to back and from side to side.

I cherry picked my favorite aspects of the technique when working with European and North American upholsterers, and I have re-worked it into the simpler method shown below, which greatly extends the life of both the springs and the burlap layer that comes later in the process. My version of the method requires no additional tacking to the frame, as it is only applied to the tops of the springs and simply adds to the stabilizing lattice effect of the lashings.

1 Work four-way lashing across the pad, as described on pages 124–126. Cut a length of laid cord 1.5 times the distance from one back corner of the pad diagonally across to the other side.

2 Make an upholsterer's slip knot (see page 97), looping it around the top coil of the spring in one corner and pulling it tight. Stretch the cord to the next spring and form a clove hitch knot, as above. Lay the cord over the intersection formed by the two previous lashes, then tie a clove hitch knot onto the other side of the top coil. Repeat as often as necessary until you get to the spring in the opposite corner. With the loose end of the cord, tie a series of half-hitch knots over the lash, from right to left, then left to right, to close off.

3 Repeat step 2 in the other diagonal direction, but where the laid cord crosses the previous diagonal lash in the gap between the springs and forms an X shape, work a clove hitch knot to lock the two lashes together and stop them from rubbing against each other with use.

4 Finish off the end of the cord with a series of half-hitches, as on the first diagonal.

At this point, the "spider's web" should mean that all of the springs are stable against each other. A simple way of checking this is to press down on any spring; every other spring in the system should move a little.

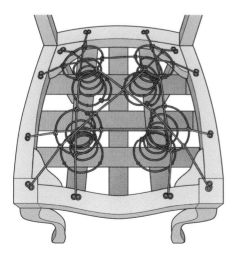

Here, the springs have been lashed from front to back, from side to side, and from corner to corner in both diagonal directions—hence the alternative name of "spider's web" lashing.

Fixing off the return ties

Return ties—the loose ends of the ties that are tacked down to the frame—are an integral part of lashing in traditional upholstery, as they tip the outer edge of the spring down toward the rail, forming the outer edges of the crown shape, and add a second fixing for greater support.

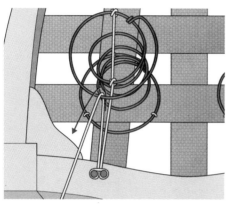

1 Take the loose end of the cord up and behind the outer edge of the top coil of the spring, over and toward you, still touching the outer edge of the wire. Bring it back down, pulling the loose end a little to tilt the outer edge of the spring down toward the frame.

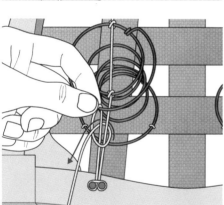

2 Tie a half-hitch knot around the cord tied to the spring as well as the loose end. When you are happy with the tilt of the spring, pull the knot tight.

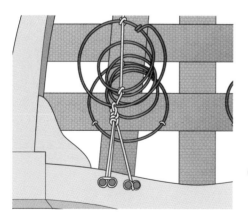

3 Repeat this half-hitch two or three times to make a strong, macramé-like rope end. Tack the loose end down to the frame.

4 Repeat on all the springs, using both ends of the twine.

Lashing serpentine springs

Lashing serpentine springs is less complicated than lashing double-cone springs.

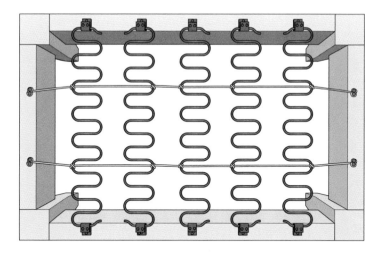

One option is to hand tie a couple of rows of clove hitch knots, using laid cord, as for double-cone springs. This may look a little amateur, but in fact it works very well.

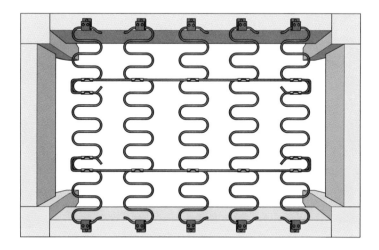

For a more professional-looking binding, use a length of spring wire long enough to bend a loop at each end that matches the loops in the two outer springs. Attach this wire to the serpentine spring by means of wire clips that are crimped into place and clamped over the two pieces of wire. In most cases, the additional wire running across the top of the serpentine springs is enough to displace the weight evenly. Alternatively, you can "whip" the wire to the springs; to do this, make a slip knot around the two wires, leaving both ends long. Use one end to make a series of knotted blanket stitches to bind the two wires together. Tie off (bind off) the end of the blanket stitches by tying the two loose ends together with two or three half-hitch knots.

An additional way of anchoring the two outer springs is to use folded lengths of webbing that are tacked onto the side rails, looped around the outer spring and fixed back onto the frame.

Setting on

Learning how to place any woven fabric—burlap, muslin (calico), the top cover—so that the weave appears square is a key skill for all upholsterers. This process is known as "setting on." If you master setting on at this stage, using inexpensive burlap, you will be in a great position later when you come to apply your expensive top-cover material.

Effectively, what you're doing is using the very obvious square weave of the fabric to create an implied X and Y axis through the center of the pad. Frames are rarely, if ever, completely square: if you follow the curves of the rails rather than the square weave of the fabric when placing the fabric layer, you may distort the pattern and/or destroy the visual impact of the rails' curves.

As you work up through the layers of the pad, treat every layer as a rehearsal for the top cover. This will not only give you a greater understanding of the shape of the frame, but it's also a fantastic way of practicing the cuts you may need to make to manipulate fabric around the rails of the frame.

With every layer, use the minimum number of tacks—three or four per side when setting on should be sufficient. Use improved tacks rather than fine, and temporary tack to begin with—don't hit them home. As you dress the panel, you may find that your original tacks were either too tight or too loose; if you temporary tack, it's easy to adjust the tension as you go.

Applying burlap

Once the springs have been knotted off, are sturdy and don't flex in any way other than straight up and down, then it is time to cover them in 12-oz (340-gram) burlap. From time to time, heavier jute canvases are marketed for this purpose; I prefer burlap, as the more open weave can flex a little better than rigid canvas—with burlap, the stitches that attach the burlap to the underlying springs can easily be worked in between the individual fibers, whereas with canvas there is a greater risk of splitting the fibers by puncturing them with the needle. Canvas is also more prone to tear over time, as the twine used for the stitches "saws" through the fibers of the fabric and breaks down the fibers.

The most important thing is to get the tension right so that the fabric is stretched evenly from side to side and from front to back of the pad. If the burlap is pulled too tight, it will compress the springs and wear though prematurely; if it is too loose, then the burlap will be baggy in between the springs and the pad will need extra stuffing to fill it out to size.

You can use either ⅜" or ½" (10-mm or 13-mm) improved tacks or ⅜" (10-mm) staples to fix this burlap layer in position. I use tacks rather than staples for temporary tacking, as they're easier to remove if I want to adjust the tension and there is less risk of damaging either the wood or the burlap. If you are using tacks for the whole process, be economical with your tack placement at this stage, as it can be frustrating later on if, every time you attempt to bang a tack in, it blunts on one underneath and hooks into the cloth rather than tacking cleanly home.

1 Cut the burlap roughly to size, adding about 3" (7.5 cm) all around, and lay it directly over the springs, ensuring that the weave is as square as possible from front to back and from side to side. Give the piece a quick pull on the bias in both directions to ensure the piece stays square.

2 Now set on the burlap. Temporary tack (drive the tacks in halfway) the burlap in place in the center of the rail that's furthest away from you, using one tack in the very center and one more on either side, about 1" (2.5 cm) apart. (If you're struggling to find the center of the frame by eye, measure it and chalk a line in the center.)

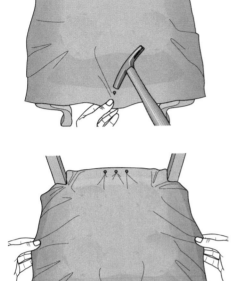

 3 Pull the burlap toward you and repeat step 2 on the rail directly opposite. If you find that you're compressing the spring as you pull the burlap, then you're pulling it too tight: the burlap should hug the top coil of the spring but not compress it downward.

4 Hold one side of the burlap in each hand and pull it toward the side rails, exerting an even tension. Repeat steps 2 and 3 on the side rails. As with the front and back rails, temporary tack rather than knock the tacks all the way into the rail. This gives you the center tension—effectively a "cross" in the center of the fabric.

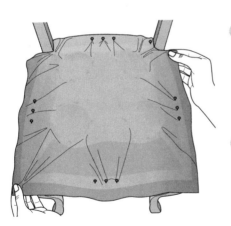

5 Now tension the fabric on the bias—repeat step 4, holding the fabric at opposite corners, and temporary tack, inserting just one tack at each corner and taking care not to distort the weave of the burlap.

6 If you're happy with the tension and the placing, knock the temporary tacks in. If not, adjust as necessary.

7 Fill in gaps between the tacks, spacing tacks about 2" (5 cm) apart. Knock in one tack, then knock in a corresponding tack on the opposite rail; this ensures that you maintain an even tension. (If you simply work along the rails, you may distort the weave.)

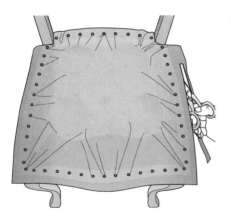

8 Following the shape of the outer edge of the rails, trim the excess burlap, leaving about 2" (5 cm) all around. Fold this surplus burlap back in toward the center of the pad and fix in place with tacks in the gaps between the first run of tacks, spacing them evenly.

Professional tip

If the weave of the burlap seems slightly distorted when you cut it off the roll, it's worth spending a few seconds manipulating it back so that it's square, by pulling the fabric in both bias directions (diagonally from corner to corner of each selvedge, in both directions).

Cutting burlap around rails

The vast majority of the upholstery students that I have met and taught find cutting into the various layers of upholstery the most daunting process. Sure enough, mistakes will occur from time to time for every upholsterer, whether he or she is just starting out or is a master of the craft—but it doesn't have to be traumatic. Learning where to place the cuts in the burlap layer is the perfect stage to have a low-risk practice at getting them right.

The majority of cuts are best approached with a bit of forethought. The layer to be cut should be folded back on itself and marked out fully in chalk before you cut it. If you have any experience of origami, you may well be at an advantage when it comes to understanding how to pre-fold materials.

The three cuts explained here will serve as a foundation for all the cutting techniques used in upholstery. They are suitable for all stages, from fitting the burlap over webbing or springs through to fitting top covers and bottoming cloth.

Single straight cut around a square rail

This is the first and least complicated cut, used principally to cut around the corners of rails where two faces meet. It is also useful for cutting around the metal bars found in iron frames and some types of spring units. Probably the most important thing to remember with this cut is that, while burlap is generally strong with a very durable warp and weft, more delicate woven fabrics are often not as strong and may be prone to tearing along the weave. The strongest direction for single straight cuts is across the bias of the fabric.

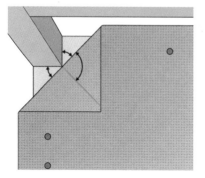

1 Set the burlap onto the frame—either directly over the top of the webbing if constructing a sprung stuffover or over the top of the springs for a sprung stuffover pad. Ensure that the warp and weft of the fabric are as square to the front and back rail as possible. Make sure that you do not tack too far along the rails so that the burlap will lay back against the rail that you are aiming to cut around.

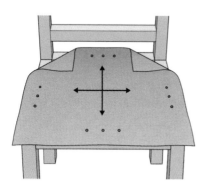

2 Fold the burlap at a 45-degree angle to the two faces of the rail that you are cutting around, making sure that the fold is just pressing against the corner of the rail. Chalk a line at 90 degrees to the fold, emanating from the point where the burlap meets the rail. If set up correctly, the chalk line should more or less follow the bias of the fabric.

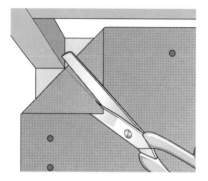

3 Cut along the chalk line as far as where the folded edge meets the rail and no farther.

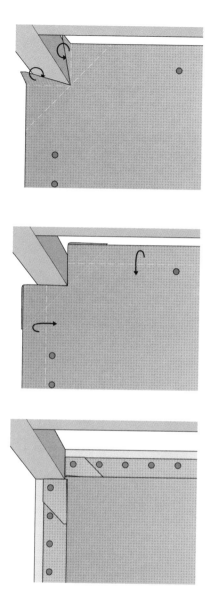

4 Fold the burlap back and under itself on either side of the cut, so the burlap now hugs the two faces of the rail that you are cutting around.

5 Tack the burlap into position and fold the raw edge back in on itself, so that the folded edge is even and not rucked up around the rail.

6 Tack the folded edge of the burlap flat.

V-cut

Cutting the burlap around the flat face of the rail uses one of the core cuts in upholstery. With two carefully placed cuts forming the "V" shape, it's relatively easy to get the burlap to mold around rails without it bunching up. Rucks in the burlap can not only make it difficult to tack off on the tacking rails with a smooth finish, but also weaken the burlap with time and form a pocket for the stuffing to gather in, leading to a dip in the surface of the completed pad.

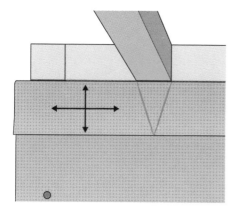

1 Temporary tack the burlap on just two rails—here, the front and back seat rails. Avoid tacking too close to the upright rails that you are intending to cut around.

2 Fold the burlap so that it butts up close to the face of the rail around which you wish to cut.

3 Mark the burlap with chalk, with the start of the chalk line right on the corner of the rail. It is important that the chalk lines are more or less diagonal and don't follow either the warp or weft of the fabric. When it is cut in this way, the burlap will be less likely to fray.

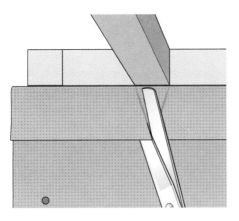

4 Cut along the chalk line, ensuring that the shears snip right up to the rail. (Don't worry if you overcut slightly, as it's actually better at this stage to be generous with your cut line.) When tacked down, the burlap will bend around the rail easily rather than stretch and create a tight pull. (V-cuts on later layers are the opposite of this, so a basic rule of thumb is as you move up through the layers and head onto the top cover, get meaner with your cuts and make them slightly shorter.)

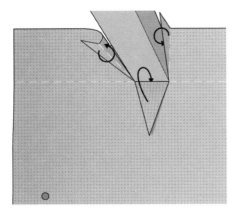

5 Fold the raw edges of the cuts back on themselves and permanently tack the burlap down on either side of the upright rail. Once you are happy that the V-cut is secure, you can tack the burlap down around all the tacking rails.

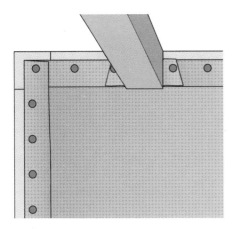

6 Trim off any excess burlap, leaving a 1" (2.5-cm) turning and tack that off all around the pad. To finish, I like to push the V-shaped tail left from the cut through to the underside of the pad, which will ensure that it doesn't get in the way of the next stages and (for slim pinstuffed pads) that there is no chance it will poke out above the finished fabric. Use a regulator to do this rather than the tip of your shears to avoid scratching the wood of the upright rail.

Y-cut

The Y-cut is an extension of the V-cut that allows the fabric to stretch around the flat faces of much wider or deeper rails. Essentially, this is a straight cut that tends to follow the warp or the weft (but not always) and then forks at the end. As with the V-cut, the cuts on later layers tend to end shy of the corners of the rail, which allows the fabric layers to bend around the faces of the rails while fitting close to the shape of the stuffing underneath. Incidentally, this also prevents the stuffing from poking out from inside the gap between the cloth and rail.

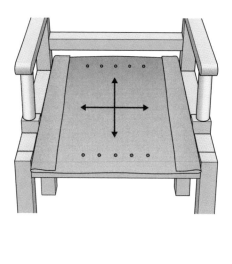

1 As for the V-cut, temporary tack the burlap on just two rails that are parallel to the faces of the rails you want to cut around.

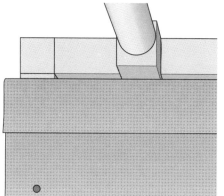

2 Fold the burlap close to the face of the upright rail. Unlike the V-cut, this time there should be a gap between the folded edge of the burlap and the tacking rail on either side of the upright rail that you are cutting around.

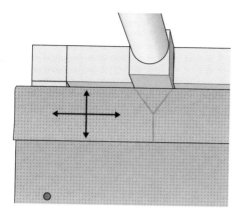

3 Chalk a V close to the rail so that the bottom or tip of the V is directly in the center of the upright rail. From this point, draw a line out to the edge of the burlap, following a single thread of the burlap as closely as you possibly can so that the straight line part of the Y is approximately 90 degrees from the face of the upright rail.

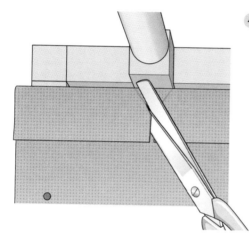

4 Once again cut along the chalk line, ensuring that the shears snip right up to the corners of the rail. If you overcut slightly at this stage it's okay—but remember it becomes very important not to overcut as you move on to the layers of cloth later on.

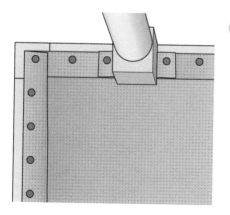

5 Fold and tack the burlap following steps 5 and 6 of the V-cut (see page 136).

Cuts on subsequent layers

Each time you add a layer of upholstery filling—for example, linen scrim over hair stuffing—the cuts will be in a similar place and will follow a similar direction to the cuts that you applied to the burlap. However, the point at which the cuts end will change. As a general rule, as the upholstery layers build up, the cuts stop farther away from the rails. Obviously the rails you are cutting around do not change in size, so for V- and Y-cuts the splay or fork of the cut doesn't widen; in fact, it usually narrows a little with each layer. The two key points to remember are:

☐ The distance between the cut and the rail that you are cutting around should be the same as the depth of the stuffing, so that the fabric pulls down tightly over and behind the stuffing; the cut then allows the fabric to sit around the rail.

☐ As well as stopping the cut farther away from the rail with each layer of stuffing, you should also reduce the width of the fork of the cut to allow the fabric to hug the stuffing as it bends around the rail.

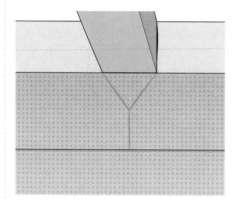

A Y-CUT ON BURLAP OVER WEBBING OR SPRINGS
The cut is close to the corners of the rail.

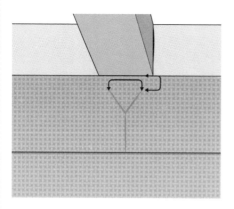

A Y-CUT ON LINEN SCRIM AFTER STUFFING
The distance from the cut to the rail is the same as the depth of the stuffing and the fork of the cut is narrower.

Stitching burlap to the top of the springs

This is a fairly simple repetition of the technique that was used to stitch the springs to the webbing below (see page 115).

I prefer to use nylon twine for stitching burlap to the springs, but threaded onto a smaller 5" (12.5-cm) curved round-point needle, rather than the heavier 6" (15-cm) bayonet needle—simply because it is much easier to get the needle through the burlap than through webbing. I work three half-hitch knots to form an open triangle shape at each spring position, with each knot gathering at least five strands of burlap. This provides more than adequate support for the stuffing layers to come, as well as locking the burlap in place.

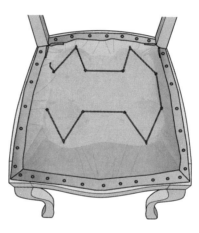

Spring units

Spring units tend to be manufactured using either cone or serpentine springs. They are certainly quicker to fit than individual springs, but they also need to be serviceable and able to flex without making a grinding noise. So, like the iron-frame furniture popular in the Victorian era, most joins are riveted or wire bound rather than welded, which keeps them tight but flexible.

Mesh-top unit

Single-cone mesh-top spring units are generally used for seats and can halve the time to fit one up to the 12-oz (340-gram) burlap stage—or more with larger seats. They are made to order. Getting the correct size in the first place is vital, as adjusting the top size after it has been manufactured can be problematic, to say the least.

Mesh-top spring units need to be a little smaller than the space they are fitting into around the edges inside the frame, but the open sides (which usually but not always means the front) need to overhang the frame by just over ½" (1 cm). This slight projection makes sitting a little more comfortable as, once padded, the unit fills the cavity behind the knee of the sitter and prevents calf muscles from rubbing against the front of the seat. The ideal gap to leave around the back and sides will vary depending on how much filling is to be applied to the top of the unit.

Mesh-top spring units are attached to the frame via holes drilled in the metal laths that support the base of the unit. Roofing felt nails called clout nails are ideal for fixing the laths in place, as they have a wide head that covers the holes in the laths generously and prevents them from pulling away from the fixings. Accurately nailing the unit to the frame takes a bit of practice.

1 First, tack or staple a thin layer of batting or a doubled piece of 12-oz (340-gram) burlap onto the top rail of the frame. This sound-dampening layer will prevent the springs from clattering on the rail each time the seat is sat on.

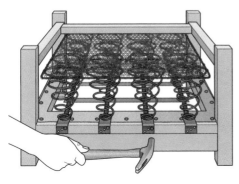

2 Next, rest the rivets at the bottom of the front row of springs on the center of the front rail and bend the lath over so that it hooks onto the frame. I advise nailing all the laths to the front of the rail and I would choose the second or third pre-drilled hole in the lath as my anchor point.

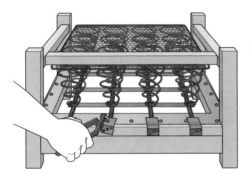

3 Once they are all fitted with one clout nail per lath, walk around the seat to the back rail. Using a pair of carpenter's pincers, grip each lath in turn as close to the frame as possible and roll the pincers so that the pressure on the lath increases and it tightens the lath. Nail this end of the laths to the frame.

4 To trim off the excess lath you will need tin snips, which are a metalworking tool. If you do not have any, then bend the end of the lath into a fold and work it back and forth; this will weaken the lath and eventually the unwanted end will snap off. Be careful not to leave sharp edges that could cut either you or the burlap covering. A swift tap with a hammer should resolve this.

5 Attach the side laths in the same way. The unit should now be firmly secured to the rail. The unit should feel flexible but not loose and, with the addition of a few lashings, will be effective for decades.

Professional tips

☐ If the holes pre-drilled in the laths are not in the ideal position, then you will need to mark the correct point for the nail hole with a marker pen when the lath is under tension and then drill the lath out; this shouldn't take long but it can be awkward if the rails in the frame are hard to access.

☐ If you find it difficult either to tighten the lath on a new unit that you're fitting or need to tighten the laths on an existing unit, crimp the lath with either a pair of pliers or hide dogs (see page 21); this effectively shortens the lath, thus tightening it up.

☐ Each of the lath ends will require two nails and wherever possible I use a nail on two faces of the rail for each lath. (This may not work on deeper front rails, but as a general rule it should work on the side and back rails.)

Lashing a mesh-top unit

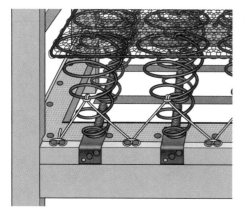

1 To lash the unit, take a length of laid cord or, more commonly, sisal no longer than the span of your arms outstretched. Starting at one end of the front row of springs, tie the spring around halfway up with a lark's foot knot tacked off onto the rail at each end. This will support the front springs in a similar way to lashes on a double-cone spring (see page 123).

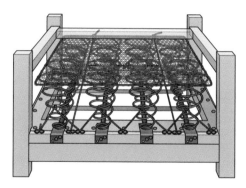

2 Once the row is finished, take a second length of cord and tie a slip knot to the top wire at the back of the mesh unit. Pull the knot tight and draw the cord forward and downward, through the unit and out of the front between the unit top and the top of the front rail and then tack or staple the cord to the top of the front rail. The cord should be tight, but not so tight that it pulls the unit forward, buckling the back of the unit and giving the seat too much projection forward over the seat rail. Front to back lashes can be applied if the lark's foot ties are not enough to prevent this from happening.

3 If the unit is slewing to one side, then a couple of lashes side to side using the same method will help to resolve it. You need two lashes per seat unit, so a chair will need a maximum of two lashes per side and a three-seat couch will require a maximum of six along the front and back of the unit and only two on each of the sides.

Applying burlap over mesh-top units

Because the mesh-top unit provides support for the burlap with more consistency than a hand-sprung base and the mesh itself is binding the top of the unit together, triangular springing stitches are not needed for this system. However, the unit does need to be stitched to the burlap and a locking blanket stitch (see page 146) is required for this. The stitch is knotted to ensure that if the twine breaks at any time there is less likelihood of the burlap loosening around the unit and a hole forming as the unit flexes up and down during use. Stitches need not be any shorter than 1" (2.5 cm) in length and once again my preferred combination is for nylon twine, using a 5" (12.5-cm) curved round-point needle.

Upholsterer's blanket stitch

An upholsterer's blanket stitch differs from a conventional embroidery blanket stitch in that it contains a half-hitch knot, rather than the thread being looped under the needle. The advantage of having a knot in each stitch is that if, at any point during the lifespan of the pad, the twine is severed or breaks, the whole row of stitching does not come undone.

Blanket stitch is used in upholstery to bind two or more objects together, be it a fabric or a structural part of the piece—for example, burlap to a spring unit. If you are using a no. 4 linen or nylon twine, the stitch length will tend to range from 1–3" (2.5–7.5 cm). If you are using waxed slipping thread in a more delicate version of the stitch, a stitch length of around ⅜" (1 cm) would be more appropriate.

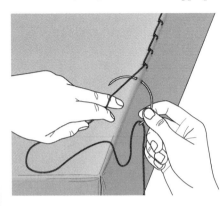 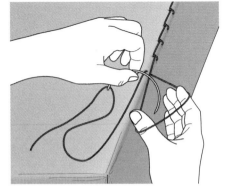

1 Using a curved needle appropriate to the size of the stitch and the thickness of the twine or thread, make a slip knot (see page 97) to start. Pass the needle through the burlap behind the edge wire and back out, forming a loop with the twine.

2 With your non-working hand, pass the needle through the loop to your other hand and draw it through.

Serpentine spring units

As the name suggests, these are constructed using serpentine or no-sag springs. The base of the unit is similar in appearance to individual springs that have been bound together with an additional wire across the seat center, but the addition of a second row of springs at the front and an edge wire clipped to them gives them a distinctive gaping fishmouth shape. As a result, they are also referred to as fishmouth units.

They are fixed to the frame using the same clips that individual serpentine springs are attached with. At the front edge, however, the wire must be aligned with the front rail so that it overhangs just a little and is a consistent height along its length. Once the base springs have all been clipped into place and the clips closed with nails or staples, this is not a challenging task.

Professional tips

☐ It's a good idea to use off-cuts of jute webbing about 12" (30 cm) long for operations like this.

☐ I fit at least one strap for every spring plus one extra strap so that the two ends are secured, too. Whenever it is possible to fix onto the side rails, I also hook a few straps around the loops of the outer springs. Three straps either side of the unit should work very well and will provide considerable strength to the unit.

☐ Do not pull the base springs quite as tight as individual springs, because the front edge wire will flex as well as the body of the seat, so the load delivered into the rails should not be so severe as with heavier-gauge individual springs.

Pocket spring units

Pocket spring units are comprised of individual barrel-shaped springs that are sewn into a cotton or synthetic sleeve and then secured into rows with hog rings. Hog rings are simply U-shaped wire clips that are crimped around two objects to join them and are most commonly used in auto trimming.

Pocket spring units have been used in upholstery principally for the interiors of cushions and were very popular throughout the early twentieth century, although they have largely been superceded by foam. The wire used in pocket springs is much thinner than that in regular seat springs, so they can create a surprisingly soft seat while maintaining a much harder, cleaner shape that is nowadays associated with foam.

Burlap covering for spring units

Spring units also need to be covered with burlap, just like individual springs (see page 131). The difference is that the burlap is blanket stitched to the edge wire of the spring unit (see page 146).

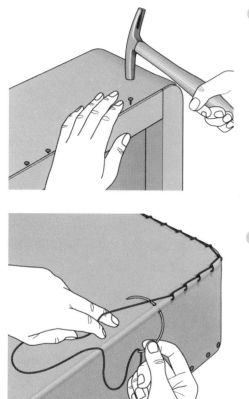

1 Secure the burlap to the frame with ⅜" (10-mm) improved tacks, folding under the raw edges.

2 Blanket stitch (see page 146) the burlap to the top edge, looping the needle under the wire of the spring unit.

Building up the pad

Chapter 4

Building up the pad

The next stage is to add the layers of fillings that build up the pad. These are the principal way of controlling the density and regulating the volume of the pad. Fillings can be divided into two categories—traditional loose and layered fillings, and modern foam and layered fillings.

Modern foam and layered fillings

This is the starting point for most people taking up upholstery for the first time. The principal advantage of using foam is that it reduces the number of layers and therefore several of the processes associated with traditional upholstery. Foam can be laid on top of either natural or elasticated webbings or springs; both require a layer of burlap in between the suspension system and the foam to prevent the pad from wearing from the inside out.

First, choose a foam density appropriate for the pad (see page 57), then decide how thick you want the foam to be.

Fitting foam

1 If you are fitting a foam pad on top of natural jute webbing or elasticated webbing covered with either a burlap layer or a modern equivalent, cut a piece of 1" (2.5-cm) thick foam measuring about half to two-thirds of the size of the frame. This piece of foam will be used to create the crown of the pad from underneath the main pad so that it is smooth and curved in appearance. Fitting this layer first is essential. Using spray adhesive, glue it to the center of the burlap. When a larger piece of foam is stretched over the top of it, the larger piece will be raised in this area, forming the crown of the pad. (This stage is not required over a sprung base, because the springs themselves will naturally form the crown.)

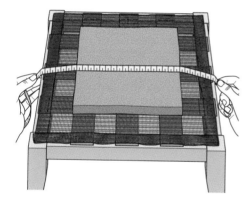

2 Measure the length and width required for the main piece of foam, then add at least ½" (1 cm) all round to compensate for the curve of the finished crown. This will also help to allow for the compression of the foam when the top-cover fabric is pulled tight. Lightly stretching a cloth tape measure over the first foam insert will achieve a more accurate measurement.

3 Glue the main piece of foam over the top of the first layer and onto the surrounding burlap.

4 Glue muslin (calico) or lining strips to either the top or the edges of the main piece of foam, then tack or staple these lining strips to the frame to get a firm fixing for the foam.

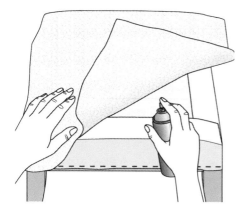

5 Glue a layer of polyester batting to the body of the foam, and staple it to the frame. For a hard, crisp, tailored look, use thin 4-oz (100-g) polyester batting. For softer, more rounded pads, use a 9–14-oz (255–400-gram) batting, which is around 1" (2.5 cm) thick. Try to avoid gluing the batting to the side of the pad as it should hang into place; if you fix it now, it may ruck up under the top cover when it is pulled tight.

6 Apply the top cover (see page 189).

Traditional loose and layered fillings

As with foam pads, preventing the various fillings from migrating or being chewed by the suspension system is an important place to start, and preventing loose filling from slipping around over the burlap base is the first stage.

Stuffing ties

Stuffing ties are loops of twine—either natural linen or nylon, depending on your preference – of a consistent depth that you create across the pad before you insert the actual filling. I tend to stick to three standard sizes of loop, based on the dimensions of my hand. (Of course, your hand may well be a different size, but the basic principle and method are still relevant.)

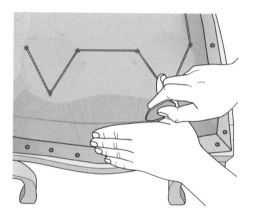

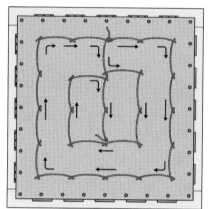

1 First, mark the position of the ties. Start by placing the little finger of your non-working hand on the edge of the frame and chalk a line a hand's width in from the edge all the way around the pad.

2 Work more lines to form a grid pattern that will be easy to follow with your stitches. Alternatively, you can simply use the width of your hand to measure as you go.

3 Thread a 4–5" (10–12.5 cm) curved round-point needle with a length of twine no longer than the span of your arms outstretched. Starting from the chalk mark farthest away from you, find the center mark and make an upholsterer's slip knot (see page 97) at this point.

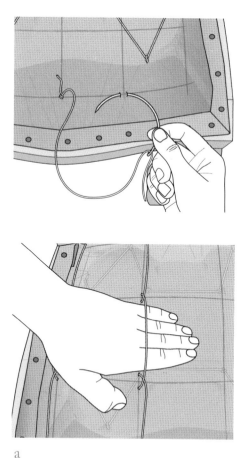

4 Measure one hand's width to one side of the knot or simply find the next chalk mark. Insert the needle into the burlap. Working back toward the slip knot, bring the needle up again no further than ⅜" (1 cm) away from the point at which you inserted it. Pull the needle through, but don't pull the twine taut. Repeat this process two or three times, working outward from the center slip knot and keeping the ties in line with each other.

5 Now you need to pull these first loops to the required size. There are three basic sizes of loop, based on easy-to-make shapes with your hand. The slimmest of these, which would give a volume suitable for a pinstuffed pad or a drop-in seat, is to lay your hand flat under the looped twine and draw the twine tight enough to just rest across your fingers (diagram a). For a slightly fuller stuffing such as a sprung dining chair, curl your fingers under toward the palm of your hand (diagram b). For a fuller stuffing still, such as a stuffover dining chair or an armchair seat, make a fist (diagram c).

a

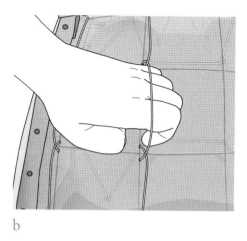

b

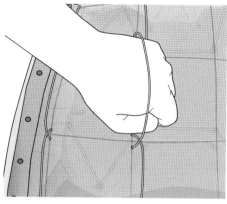

c

To keep all the ties in line with each other, follow one thread of the burlap across; because the weave is so open, this is easy to see. Alternatively, chalk a line across the burlap.

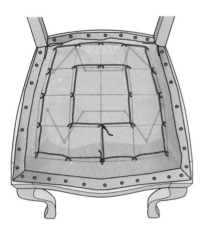

6 Repeat these steps around the outer edge of the pad, maintaining a line that's either a hand's width in from the edge or follows the guidelines marked out earlier, until you get back to the original slip knot. Then turn the direction of the stitches and work in toward the center of the pad, either by following the center line across the middle of the pad or by making another circuit of the pad a hand's width apart at a time. It can be tempting to flood the pad with rows and rows of stuffing ties, but they can get in the way later on when you are trying to wrestle handfuls of stuffing into adjacent rows.

7 Go round and check the depth of all the ties again to make sure they're consistent and adjust if necessary. If some ties are noticeably deeper than others, you'll end up with a very uneven stuffing.

(There are some exceptions to this: if you want to create a domed crown, for example, you would make the ties at the side of the pad deeper than those in the center, whereas if you want to create a flat pad over a sprung base, you might want to do the opposite and make the ties shallower over the crown.)

8 Once all the heights have been fixed, bind off the twine by tying off a series of half-hitch knots (see page 98) after the last stuffing tie.

Note: Confusingly, you may hear some upholsterers referring to this type of tie as a bridle tie—and vice versa. This can cause quite heated debates! I always call them stuffing ties—for the very simple reason that they tie in the stuffing!

Patterns for stuffing ties

Different pad shapes and sizes require different numbers and arrangements of stuffing ties in order to secure the filling. There are no hard-and-fast rules, but space the ties evenly and work consistently in a clockwise or anticlockwise direction, so that you're not going back and crossing over previously stitched ties, running the risk of tangling the twine and preventing the tie from expanding as the stuffing is placed under it. As in most of the techniques I have described, spacing the rows of stuffing ties a hand's width apart will provide a sufficient gap without them being too far apart to provide enough anchorage for the fillings.

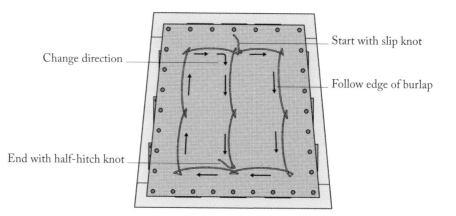

Change direction

Start with slip knot

Follow edge of burlap

End with half-hitch knot

STANDARD TIE PATTERN FOR A SMALL SQUARE PAD
SUCH AS A DROP-IN SEAT
The ties are spaced roughly one hand's width apart around the outside of the pad, with three equidistant ties down the center.

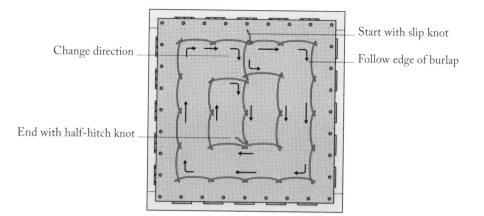

Change direction

Start with slip knot

Follow edge of burlap

End with half-hitch knot

TIE PATTERN FOR A LARGER SQUARE PAD

This is typical of larger seats found in chairs for lounging in rather than perching on—for example, an armchair rather than a normal dining chair. Here, there is a square of stuffing ties in the center of the pad; this will help to keep the stuffing in the crown of the seat and prevent it from drifting to the outside of the pad with use.

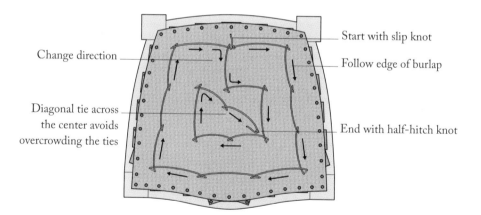

Change direction

Start with slip knot

Follow edge of burlap

Diagonal tie across the center avoids overcrowding the ties

End with half-hitch knot

TIE PATTERN FOR A LARGER TAPERED PAD

This might be found in large carver dining chairs and armchairs where the front is wider than the back. The additional tie across the center of the pad also helps to keep the crown fully formed.

Preparing the first stuffing

On a microscopic level, all loose fibers are slightly barbed—so after being stuffed into a sack and transported, they will settle and slightly knit together. Never underestimate the value of teasing the fibers apart manually to restore their springiness. This also gives you the chance to pull out and discard any matted lumps.

Professional tip

If you're doing this at home, lay a sheet over your carpet or flooring—the loose fibers get everywhere and are very difficult to get rid of just by vacuuming.

1 Start by pulling off large handfuls or balls of the teased-out stuffing material, keeping them as consistent in size as possible. I like to put the fingertips of my two hands together to form a kind of cage, and then pull off the amount of stuffing that will fill the "cage." This makes it much easier to keep the density of stuffing consistent across the pad when you begin to insert it under the stuffing ties. As a very rough guide, you will need two such handfuls for a flat-hand stuffing tie, three for a knuckle-depth tie and four for a fist-depth tie.

Professional tip

Close your eyes as you do this, so that you're relying on touch and the feel of the stuffing rather than trying to do it by sight.

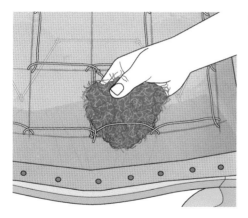

2 I find that the easiest way to keep the shape of the pad while stuffing is to fill the ties around the outer edges of the pad first—rather like building a retaining wall, this helps to prevent the stuffing from spilling out over the edges of the frame. Take your handful of stuffing and push it under the tie from the inside to the outside. This gives a smoother outer edge to the stuffing, as the fibers tend to catch on the burlap and bunch up as you slide the stuffing across it.

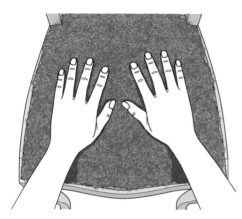

3 Work your way around the rows of stuffing ties until you've worked right into the middle of the pad. Lay your hands flat on the pad and feel for any bumps or gaps in the stuffing.

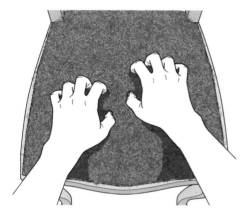

4 Before you add or take away any stuffing, use your fingertips to tousle the stuffing; lock your fingers in position, then move your arms gently to fluff up the fibers and knit them together. Don't overwork it, though, as you don't want to compress and compact the fibers.

5 If there are still gaps or lumps left, remove or add small amounts of stuffing where necessary.

Covering the first stuffing with linen scrim

Linen scrim is used to encase the stuffing and form the shape of the pad. To work out the size of scrim required, simply drape a cloth tape measure over the stuffing, so that the end is touching the work surface. Pull the tape measure tight over to the other side of the pad. Do this in both directions. Add 4" (10 cm) all around.

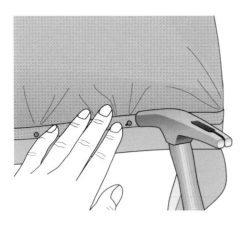

1 Chalk out the scrim and cut it to size. It is advisable to cut your scrim 3–4" (7.5–10 cm) larger than your measurement all the way around; as you get used to this process, the amount can be cut down but being unnecessarily mean with your allowance is rarely an advantage. Using ⅜" (10 mm) improved tacks, set on the scrim, following the same basic method as for the 12-oz (340-gram) burlap (see page 130) – but instead of tacking the scrim onto the top of the rail, temporary tack it onto the outer edge of the rail. If the scrim comes off the tacks, fold it double where you're tacking. Remember: you only need three or four tacks in each rail to hold the central tension. Be careful not to pull it so tight that you crush the stuffing and end up with a very thin pad.

2 If you are struggling to see the shape of the pad with just the tension across the center of the scrim, put in one or two temporary tacks at the corners, so that the scrim is stretched on the bias. You can now start marking out the position of the bridle ties.

Professional tips

☐ To get a straight line in the linen scrim, snip through the selvedge across a couple of threads, splay the snip open, and pull one thread like a drawstring. Cut across the thread and remove it. This gives a gap in the weave, which you can cut along with your scissors.

☐ Remember that, as you work up through the layers, any cuts around rails should end farther away from the rails than in the burlap layer (see page 133).

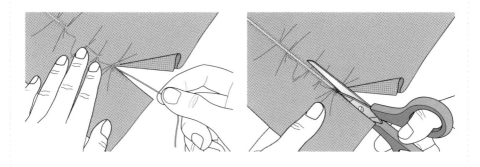

Bridle ties

Bridle ties are long stitches that bind the top layer of scrim to the base burlap, sandwiching the stuffing between them and allowing the surface of the scrim to be made level, so that the base for the second stuffing is even and consistent. Although it is often described as being similar to a running stitch, I was taught early on to never rely on that method and instead always knot each tie with a simple half-hitch knot. This also allows me to control the depth of the pad I am constructing, depending on how tight I pull each individual knot.

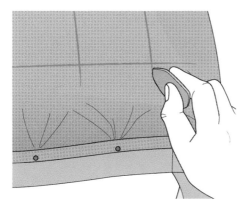

1. Chalk a line around the linen scrim, loosely following the pattern of the stuffing ties (see page 155): measure in by at least one hand's width and follow a straight line along the weave. I advise chalking a line more than one hand's width in from the edge, so that the ties do not clash or tangle with the blind stitches that will be applied later (see page 170).

2 Take a length of no. 4 linen or nylon twine no longer than the span of your arms outstretched. Thread a straight round-point buttoning needle. (For most applications, a 10" (25-cm) needle is most suitable.)

3 Working from the top of the pad, make a slip knot (see page 97), drawing the needle through the scrim, the stuffing and the 12-oz (340-gram) burlap underneath the stuffing. Bring the needle straight up through all layers, about ⅜" (1 cm) away from where it emerged. Pull the twine to slide the slip knot up close against the scrim, pulling it just tight enough to form a dimple in the scrim surface.

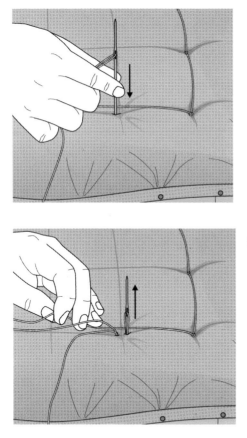

4 At the next marked point, insert the needle again vertically through all layers.

5 Take it back in the direction from which you've come by ½–¾" (1–2 cm), and bring it back up to the top surface, drawing the needle completely out of the pad.

6 Take the needle under the thread from the previous stitch, passing it through once and draw it tight to form a half-hitch knot (see page 98). Repeat around the pad, following the same pattern as the stuffing ties described earlier, and bind off in the same way (see page 157).

☐ When you first bring the needle up, it's advisable to give both ends of the twine a tug and to look underneath to make sure that the twine has hooked around the burlap. If you're working on a sprung seat, make sure you haven't caught any of the spring coils in this stitch, as this will tug on the spring and reduce the lifespan of the stitch.

☐ If you're struggling to get the needle through the burlap as well as the scrim and the stuffing, adjust the angle of the needle very slightly from the vertical as you pull it through to the underside: you will hear a small "pinging" sound as it slips through the burlap.

Tacking off the scrim

Before you set the final scrim position, take a moment or two to adjust the quantity of hair or fiber filling in order to achieve the desired volume and density.

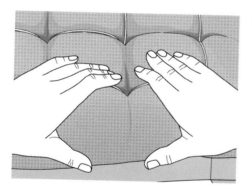

1 Using a tack lifter or ripping chisel, knock out the temporary tacks that you used to set on the scrim on one edge of the pad. Position your thumb at right angles to the palm of your hand and push in against the edge of the pad, checking that the stuffing is both consistent in density and in the right place. Add or remove stuffing as required to get a firm edge of stuffing around the pad.

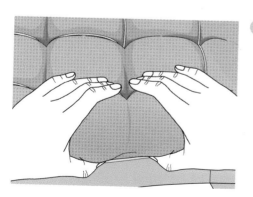

2 Once you're happy with the stuffing, use your thumbs to push the edge of the scrim under the stuffing.

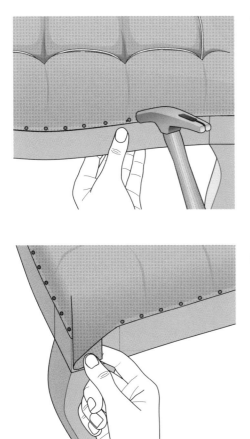

3 Using fine tacks rather than improved, as they have a smaller head that is less likely to be felt through the top cover, tack the scrim down onto the bevel between the front and top faces of the rail. Space the tacks around 1" (2.5 cm) apart. You can add more tacks later on prior to stitching once you've determined the overall shape by tacking off the scrim. Tack down the middle two-thirds of all four rails to begin with, then tackle the corners.

4 Release any temporary tacks on the corners. Pull the scrim that you tucked under the stuffing, as if you're fitting a flat sheet over a mattress—rather like a "hospital corner." On the adjoining side, fold the fullness of the scrim in on itself, then tuck it under in the same way, so that you get a neat join between the two edges.

5 Tack off the scrim as before, holding the pleat in the scrim in place with a couple of upholstery skewers.

Professional tip

Tap the corner tacks in gently. You're now tacking into the end grain of the wood over the leg of the piece, rather than along the grain, and if you tap too hard you may chip out small chunks of wood rather than getting the tack to bite.

---

6 Repeat on all corners, making sure that you fold the scrim in the same way on each one, so, for example, if you fold the side edge of the scrim in before the front edge on the first corner, do the same on subsequent corners.

Regulating the stuffing

Regulators are used to manipulate loose fillings and distribute them throughout a pad—hence the name "regulator." When regulating, you have to think about the correct density of filling for the piece as a whole, rather than just concentrating on one very small area. You may, for example, come across a loosely filled area in between two more dense sections: what you have to ask yourself is whether it's the loose or the more tightly packed section that is the "correct" density.

Regulators can be held in a variety of ways. The most common are as follows:

Hand clasped around the flat eye

This is the best way to hold the regulator when shifting fillings around underneath the scrim. Holding the regulator in this way should prevent your arm from tiring quickly during a prolonged bout of regulating. Use your thumb to act as a depth gauge so that each movement is catching a similar amount of filling. By inserting the regulator through the open weave of the scrim and moving your wrist, you are able to either drag the filling toward you or push it away to fine-tune the filling placement and density.

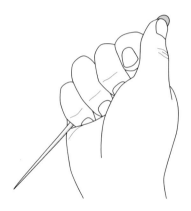

Thumb on the flat eye

This is the correct way to hold the regulator when inserting additional stuffing into the pad via the gap left in the scrim parallel to a rail.

Once you have finished regulating the pad and are satisfied that the density and volume are correct, the scrim should have large gaps in the weave where the insertion and rocking/twisting of the regulator will have distorted the weave. If left unresolved, these gaps will allow the fibers to migrate into the upper layers, so should be "dressed" back into place by lightly dragging the flat end of the regulator many times over the surface of the scrim, following the direction of both the wrap and the weft threads. This also helps to retain the graph-paper effect of the weave, which helps to keep it square and helps you to understand the shape and dimensions of the pad.

Edge-stitching techniques

Stuffings alone cannot hold their shape indefinitely, so various stitches are applied to support the stuffing and build the edge of a pad so that it retains its shape. This is a vital element of producing a sturdy, yet comfortable, piece of furniture and one of the most important processes of traditional upholstery.

If you haven't yet marked out your frame (see page 92), now is the time to do so.

In traditional upholstery, edge stitches fall into two main categories: blind stitch and top stitch. Each stitch plays a specific role.

The principal role of blind stitch is to build height into the edge of the pad. Sadly I can't give you an easy-to-remember thickness that all pads should be blind stitched to, but provided the pad has been well stuffed, a good rule of thumb is that for every ¾" (2 cm) height of stuffing that you've inserted, you should work one row of blind stitch.

Top stitches, as the name suggests, sit above the top blind stitch and are how you begin to define the edge of the pad. It is usual to use either one or two rows of top stitch, depending on how well defined you want the edge to look.

Like blind stitch, a top stitch will secure around ¾" (1–2 cm) of stuffing height. So a couple of rows of blind stitches building up a solid foundation and a row of top stitch defining the edge top will make a pad around 2½" (6 cm) high, which is the thickness at which most dining seat pads begin. If you want to form a pad that is thinner than this, a combination of a single row of blind stitches and a slightly thinner top stitch will be suitable for a finished pad thickness of up to 1½" (4cm).

If you are looking to create a deeper, fuller edge to your pad and make something that is 4" (10 cm) high or even more, my advice is to build up the height with blind stitches and finish off the top of the pad with two rows of top stitches.

Needles and twine for edge stitching

The needle size is dictated by the depth of the pad that you're intending to stitch and whether or not there are any leg posts, arms or a back that make it difficult to access the scrim. Generally, a 10" (25-cm) or 12" (30-cm) straight needle should be fine. Deeper pads may need a longer needle—and if you reach a point where a straight needle is not helping you to form the stitches, then you should consider using a large curved needle. If you have no curved needles long enough, you can bend a straight one to form a curve—but do take care to not break the needle as you may cut yourself in the process. I prefer round-point needles with a point on each end, as they won't cut the scrim as you draw the needle back and forth through the pad.

Nylon twine is commonly used today due to its great strength. It also slips through the stuffing easily and is less likely to snag itself as you pull the stitch tight. No. 4 linen twine is the traditional choice for edge stitching, but it has a tendency to snag. Applying beeswax to the twine before you start has two benefits. As the needle and twine are drawn through the pad the friction is reduced, resulting in the twine being less likely to snag; and once the stitch is in place, the wax helps to set the stitch and reduces the likelihood of the stitch tension slipping.

Ultimately it's down to you to try out what is available. Good-quality natural twines and nylon twines tend to be around the same cost, but solid beeswax can be tough to get hold of at a reasonable price. At a push, you can use ordinary paraffin-wax candles to lubricate linen twine, but they won't set the knot as well as natural beeswax.

Blind stitch

I cannot pretend that there is only one way to blind or top stitch, as I have seen upholsterers produce a great many ways of creating these stitches. However, the method shown below is tried and tested.

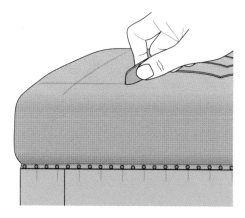

1 Draw a chalk line directly onto the scrim all around the top face of the pad, about 4" (10 cm) or a hand's width in from the edge, making sure that the line doesn't come inside the bridle ties. This is where the needle should come out when it is drawn through the pad, thus helping to ensure that the same amount of stuffing is contained by each stitch. This line should not cross over the bridle ties, as it will cause the blind stitch to snag the bridle ties. If it does, it is best to cut the bridle ties and re-position them farther into the pad before you proceed any further.

Do remember to regulate the stuffing (see page 167) just ahead of making your stitches. I usually regulate the stuffing for two or three stitches at a time and then stitch the stuffing I have just regulated and repeat that cycle around the pad and for each row of stitches.

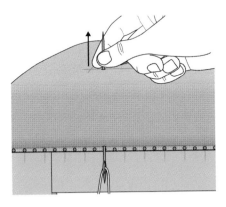

2 To start your row of blind stitching, line the needle up with either a tack or your first mark drawn on the frame (see page 92), or if you are working on a square frame such as a foot stool start a little way in along one edge to avoid starting close to a corner. Push the unthreaded end of the needle up through the pad and out of the top, emerging on the chalk line that you drew in the previous step, and drawing it out just far enough for you to see the eye.

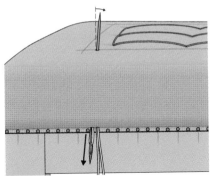

3 Change the angle very slightly so that the needle will virtually follow the same path, then push the needle back through the pad and out of the side, so that it comes out around ¼" (5 mm) back from the entry point but at the same height up from the wood. Draw the needle all the way out and unthread it to help avoid getting tangled up.

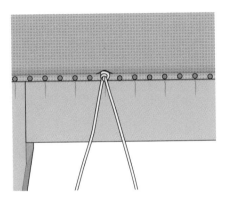

4 Make an upholsterer's slip knot (see page 97), which will serve as an anchor for the row. Draw the knot up to the scrim and then tighten it carefully. The ideal tension is enough to hold the stuffing while drawing it forward slightly and pulling the side of the scrim in a little, but be careful to not overtighten the knot and make the scrim on the edge pull too deeply into the pad. As with all slip knots, use your thumb nail to help the knot slide up to the pad as you tighten it.

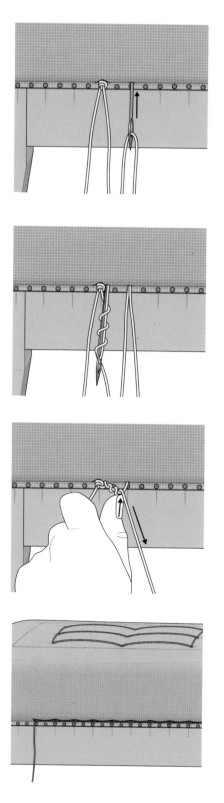

5 Re-thread the needle with the twine. Using the chalk marks on the frame as a guide. Line your next stitch up 1" (2.5 cm) farther along and push the needle straight into the pad, aiming for the guideline on the top of the pad. As with the slip knot in steps 2 and 3, draw the needle up so that the threaded eye is just showing, then angle the needle slightly and head back out to the side of the pad, bringing the needle out just in front of the slip knot in line with the mark on the frame.

6 The eye of the needle should be poking out of the side by about 3" (7.5 cm). Twist the longest thread trailing from the slip knot around the needle three times, then draw the needle completely out of the pad. Nylon twine has a tendency to untwist itself and fall off the needle; to avoid this, lightly hold it to the needle while you draw the needle out.

7 Using your thumb, slip the twists up along the thread and pull the stitch tight, using the tension you achieved on the slip knot as a guide. Squeezing the fillings with your left hand may help to achieve the correct tension, too. Make the second stitch in the same way, bringing the needle out of the side of the pad through the hole created at the start of the previous stitch.

8 Repeat this process around the edge. Keeping the stitch length even and aiming for the chalk line on the top of the pad will help ensure that the same volume of stuffing is held with the same tension, this will give the pad an even density.

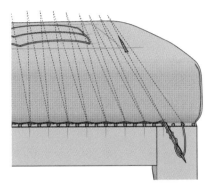

9 At the corners, as the needle comes through the top, reduce the distance to the previous exit hole on the top face of the pad along the chalk line, while keeping to your guideline marks on the side; this creates a "fan" shape that evenly distributes the pull of the stitches and will help to avoid a lopsided corner, in which all the stuffing is pulled to one side.

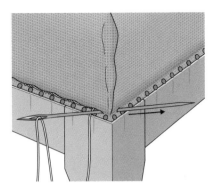

10 When you get to the corner itself, simply pass the needle through the corner, effectively cutting the corner off to prevent the thread from crushing the stuffing, and then carry on as though you had put a full stitch in.

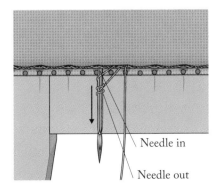

Needle in

Needle out

11 To finish (or "bind off") a row of blind stitching, simply make sure the last stitch butts up close to the slip knot that started the row of stitching, and put a second stitch directly over the top of the last stitch by inserting the needle into the same entry and exit holes made during the previous stitch.

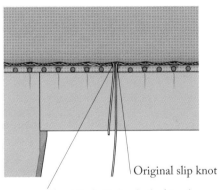

Original slip knot

Two blind stitches locked in place

12 Draw the knot tight, using your thumb to help form the twists as before. This second stitch will effectively lock itself over the top of the first stitch and prevent the stitches from slipping loose during the next stages. Try to avoid the twists bunching up as you pull the knot tight, as this can form a lump that may be felt through the finished pad.

Starting a new length of twine

Running out of twine as you go along is an everyday occurrence; it is virtually impossible to calculate the exact length of twine you need per run of stitching. If you hold one end of the twine in one hand, the ball in your other and spread your arms out wide, that should give you an idea as to the maximum length of twine for your body size to work with. Starting a new length is fairly simple—but don't just knot the ends of the old and new twines together, as the stitching may need to be adjusted later on.

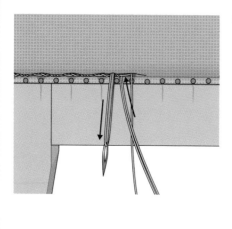

1 Re-thread the needle with twine, insert it just under the center of your last blind stitch and draw the needle out on the chalk line on the top of the pad. Then change the angle very slightly so that you can push the needle back through and come out on the side of the pad, just above the twists of the blind stitch.

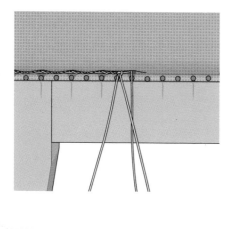

2 Tie a slip knot and pull it tight, so that it clamps over your last stitch in the run and locks it in place, and then carry on as though the twine is part of the original length that started the row.

Second and subsequent rows of blind stitch

Starting the second row of blind stitches around ⅜" (1 cm) above the previous row will add around ⅝" (1.5 cm) additional structure, thickness, and definition to the edge of an upholstered pad. You can make an informed decision about increasing the gaps between rows of stitching, but be warned: any gap over 1" (2.5 cm) could potentially result in the edge of the pad being softer, leading to a much shorter lifespan for the edge of the pad.

Original chalk line

Second blind stitch line

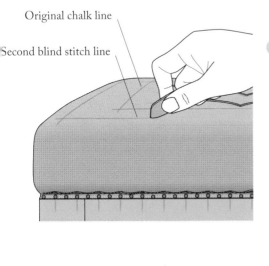

1 Start by chalking a second line on the top of the pad, parallel to the first one but 1" (2.5 cm) closer to the outer edge of the pad.

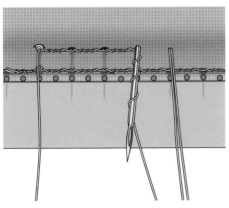

2 Start stitching the second row of blind stitches at about ⅜" (1 cm) above the previous row to give an additional thickness of around ⅝" (1.5 cm) to the pad. As for the first row, start with a slip knot. Stitch the whole way around the pad, joining new lengths of twine where necessary and binding off the end using the method as described on page 173. Don't forget to regulate the stuffing ahead of every few stitches.

Professional tips

☐ Matching the corner shape of the pad to the shape of the frame is vital. If the frame at the top of the leg is rounded, the row of stitching should show on the outside all the way around the pad. If the corner is sharp, however, stopping just shy of it and passing the needle through the pad (behind the leg) from one edge to another creates a sharp, right-angled corner.

☐ Unless your row starts directly next to a leg or rail of some kind, staggering the starting point of a row will help to even the tension out around the pad and avoid loading too much strain on just a few strands of the scrim where the slip knots pull in.

☐ If the scrim has been cut around an upright rail, take care to not overtighten the first slip knot in each row of blind stitching, as this can form a cavity in the pad where the slip knots pull against the linen scrim.

Top stitch

Top stitches are worked in a similar way to blind stitches, but their role is to define the edge of the pad rather than to build up height. The final row of top stitching should have two stitches to every stitch below it. If you are intending to put one row of top stitches into the pad, for example, then halve the length of the stitch compared to the blind stitches. If you intend to work two rows of top stitches, work the stitches in the first row to the same length as the blind stitches and then reduce the stitch length of the second row of top stitches. This will be simple if you follow the marks made on the frame. Regulating the fillings ahead of the stitches at this stage is also an important way of ensuring that the edge of the pad has a consistent density and shape. As with blind stitches, it is much easier to form the stitches if the fillings have been regulated into place and the stitches are supporting the filling rather than pulling them into shape.

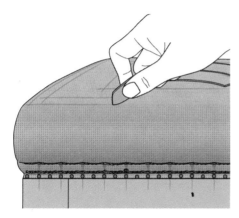

1 Draw another chalk line directly onto the scrim on the top face of the pad, running parallel to the previous chalk line used for the second row of blind stitch, 1" (2.5 cm) closer to the outer edge of the pad.

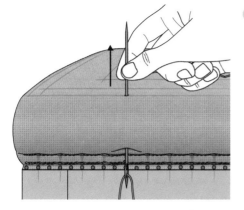

2 Starting your row of top stitching is very similar to the start of the blind stitch. Make sure you have regulated the edge stuffing to form a firm roll and then line the needle up with a mark on the frame. Once again don't be afraid to stagger the starting point if working on a stool top, but you may have to line the slip knot up with the slip knot on the blind stitch row below. Push the unthreaded end of the needle up through the pad, ensuring that it comes through the top of the pad on the most recently marked chalk line. Draw it all the way out this time.

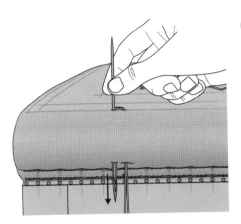

3) Staying on the chalk line, move the needle to the left by ½" (12 mm), then push the needle back into the pad following the same trajectory. Bring it back out of the side of the pad, around ½" (12 mm) from the entry point but at the same height up from the previous row of blind stitching.

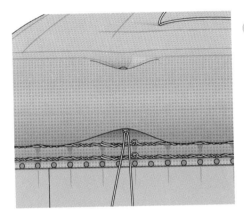

4) Once again make an upholsterer's slip knot (see page 97), which will serve as an anchor for the row. Unlike the blind stitches, the starting knot of the top stitches will pinch the scrim around the fillings and start to form a defined edge.

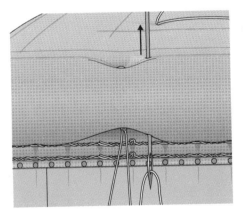

5) Using both the chalk marks on the frame and the previous rows of blind stitches as a guide, halve the distance before you insert the needle back into the pad.

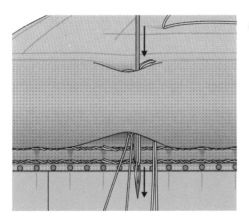

6 Just as you did with the slip knot, draw the needle up and completely out of the pad at the chalk line. Move the needle back along the chalk line, re-insert it into the hole made by the slip knot, push it back into the pad and bring it out on the side of the pad close to the slip knot, at the same height up from the blind stitch row below.

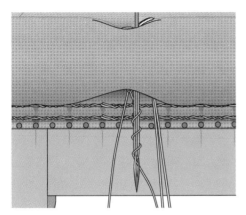

7 Wind the thread trailing from the slip knot around the needle three times. It is important to wind the correct thread around the needle—make sure you wind the thread attached to the previous knot and not the loose end. This ensures that the twine doesn't bunch up as the stitch is pulled tight and form tight balls of twine under the finished roll.

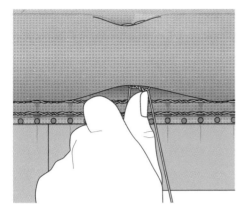

8 Pull the needle completely out of the pad and draw the thread tight in the same way as for blind stitch, using your thumbnail to chase the twist along the twine as the stitch is formed.

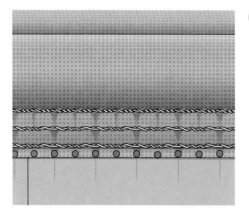

9 Repeat this process around the edge, keeping the stitch length the same and ensuring that you regulate the fillings ahead of the stitch so that the amount of stuffing being gathered up by the top stitches is consistent. The need to regulate fillings ahead of either blind or top stitches really cannot be overstated, however tedious it may feel at the time.

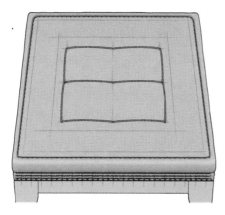

10 Going around the corner is much easier for a top stitch, as you maintain the method and stitch length on the top of the pad and simply let the twine run around the edge of the corner rather than trying to pass the needle through. This may result in the stitch around the edge appearing longer than the regular stitches; this is normal, so do not worry.

11 Continue until all four sides have been stitched, joining in new lengths of twine where required and binding off in the same way as for blind stitch (see page 173).

Professional tip

If two rows of top stitches are required, try to make sure they are spaced evenly up from the blind stitches and in from the edge, so that the depth of stitch and the overall density of the edge roll are the same throughout.

Second stuffing

A second stuffing gives you the opportunity to create a softer layer of filling on top of the now rigid stitched pad. It also gives you a chance to adjust the shape. For example, if the pad is too thin or flat, you can put in additional stuffing to thicken it or create more of a domed shape in the crown. The more diligent you are in preparing the filling used in a second stuffing, the more comfortable and durable it will be.

1 Using a curved needle, apply shallow (finger-tight) stuffing ties to the scrim layer only (see page 156).

2 Prepare and insert the stuffing (see page 160). While the second stuffing should not be overstuffed or overhang (looking rather like a muffin), as the overhanging stuffing could quickly become lumpy with use, don't scrimp on the amount of stuffing you use.

Muslin (calico)

Instead of covering the stuffing with burlap, use muslin (calico), allowing enough extra all around to tack down onto the frame. The fabric will contain the loose fillings and help the pad to maintain a full appearance.

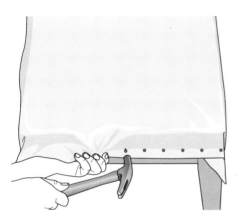

1 Cut the fabric to size and set it on (see page 130), keeping the warp and the weft as square to the front of the chair as possible.

2 Fold the fabric, ensuring the fold line is along the bias when intending to cut around the point of a rail where a single cut will be used (see page 134), or fold the fabric flat against the faces of any arm rails, as with the burlap and the scrim layers. Remember to make an allowance for the thickness of the pad. When applying either straight or Y-cuts (see pages 134 and 138), don't chalk out the cut line as close to the leg or arm rails.

Professional tips

Getting the balance between enough filling and too much can take some practice. Don't feel rushed: letting the stuffing rest for a day or two, possibly even laying a good-sized hardback book with a weight on to compress the fillings once the muslin (calico) has been set on before you go on to the next stage, is rarely a waste of time. It's better to invest a few hours here and potentially add years to the life of the pad than to regret an underfilled pad that compresses within months of being used.

This is the last opportunity to rehearse these cuts before you put the top cover on, so if you are not sure, practice the cuts on some scraps of fabric.

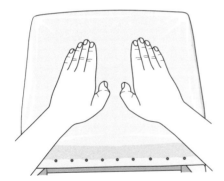

3 Carefully increase the tension in the muslin (calico) and tack it to the side of the rails. To check if the tension is correct, place your hands flat on the top of the pad. Pressing down firmly, tucking your thumbs in, and slide your hands together until they meet.

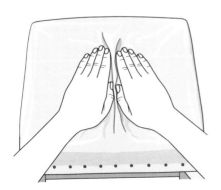

4 If any fabric gathers up and is trapped in between, the tension is still too loose. Remove tacks, adjust the tension and check again until there is no further fabric movement.

If the rail is very thin and the tacking area is limited, or if the age and condition of the rails is poor, rather than setting on the muslin (calico) by temporary tacking it to the frame, use upholstery skewers to secure it in place.

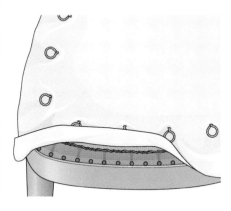

1 Push the skewers through the muslin (calico) and into the outer edge of the top stitching.

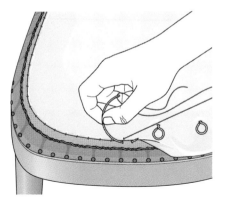

2 Trim off the excess fabric below the skewers, leaving 1" (2.5 cm). As when turning under the scrim (see page 165), use your thumbs or the flat end of the regulator, working on opposite edges in turn and re-skewering the turned-under edge as you go. Slipstitch (see page 214) the fabric to the pad.

This method is also more suited to pads with irregular-shaped edges, where tacking would result in the muslin (calico) forming into a multitude of tiny pleats and gathers.

Battings,
top cover & trims

Chapter 5

Battings, top cover & trims

Batting

The next stage is to apply batting to add a level of softness directly under the cover that cannot be achieved from the filling used to build the structure of the pad. In traditional upholstery, this is done over the muslin (calico) layer; in modern upholstery, it is done directly over the foam.

Batting is a term given to softer layered fillings, but can be broken into two distinct groups: materials that add volume but also prevent the migration of fibrous fillings (felt battings) and materials that provide a consistent level of softness directly under the cover (polyester batting). Recent developments in battings have hinged around the idea of making 100% wool battings that can fulfill both roles.

Applying batting

Types of batting are discussed on pages 54–63. Your choice of which batting to use is determined by several factors, including softness and cost, but regardless of the one you choose, there are similarities in the way they are applied and in the finished result. You can apply several layers in order to build up the volume of the pad, although they do compress with use.

1. Measure over the top of the muslin (calico). For layered and wool/cotton felts, using your hands rather than scissors, roughly break off the amount of material you need from the roll, allowing a few inches extra. Most cotton felt rolls are 27" (68 cm) wide, so you will need to butt pieces together. Skin batting, polyester batting and needled/bonded felts need to be cut with scissors. Needled and bonded felts are difficult to cut through and only heavy-duty 10" or 12" (25- or 30-cm) shears will do the job with ease.

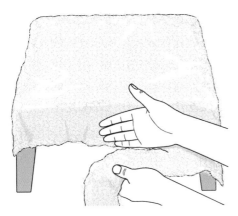

2. Lay the batting on the area you want to cover. If you're working on an open pad, such as a stuffover seat, hold the edge of the batting in one hand and "chop" through it with your working hand to tear it away from the edge of the pad; this feathers the edge of the batting and helps to retain the overall shape of the pad. Controlling the amount you allow to overhang is a useful way of either building the edge of the pad out or making it squarer on the edge.

3. Tousle the edges of felt pieces together with your fingers using a similar technique as for horsehair and coir stuffings (see page 161) to "blur" the join between pieces and prevent them from drifting apart during use.

Professional tip

If you're using cotton felt, it's best not to physically tack it to the frame or glue it to the pad at any stage, because that may cause it to ruck up as the cover is pulled tight. Bonded black felt and needled felt have a stiff backing, so they can be tacked or glued.

4. If the volume of the pad is still too thin, this is your chance to build it up by applying a second layer of batting. However, this layer too needs to be feathered out at the edges – if it overhangs too much, it will distort the line along the top edge of the pad. Trimming off any excess batting under the arms or back can be done from the other side of the chair. Again, just pull off any excess, feathering the edges as in step 2.

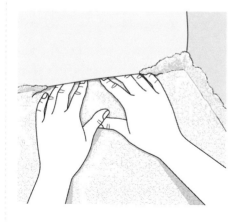

Fitting felt batting over a seat pad that is enclosed by back and arms can be tricky; many newcomers to upholstery struggle to tuck it down into the gap between the panels without tearing the layer or gathering the batting, thus changing its density. I find the easiest way of managing this is to splay your fingers out as wide as you can and use your fingertips to first compress the batting and then your whole hand to gently push the batting down into the gap.

Applying polyester batting

Fitting polyester batting to a pad needs to be approached with care, as any foreign particles or inconsistencies in the polyester will invariably be felt through the top cover. Polyester batting should be lightly fixed onto the frame with the bare minimum of fixings (to prevent it from rucking up under the cover when it gets pulled tight). In contrast to most layers of upholstery, don't be too generous when measuring for polyester batting and possibly even be a little mean as the thinner battings will often stretch when fitted.

Fire-retardant linings

Anyone upholstering commercially or intending to sell upholstery must ensure that the layer directly beneath the top cover complies specifically with the fire regulations in force where the furniture is being sold.

Fire-retardant linings fall into two main categories: muslin (calico) that has been impregnated with fire-retardant chemicals, and linings woven using either natural or man-made materials, or a combination of the two that are inherently fire retardant. The latter are often slightly thicker and slightly fluffy in feel, so perform a little more like a polyester batting under the top cover. These are usually used in conjunction with a top-cover upholstery fabric that does not comply with fire regulations. Note that conventional polyester batting is NOT a fire-retardant barrier.

Top cover

Provided you took careful notes when ripping down, you'll be able to tell which pieces were laid over others; this in turn will enable you to tell which pad was upholstered first. Like many upholsterers in the United Kingdom, when upholstering a full chair or couch, I generally start by constructing the arm pads first and then cover them before moving on to the inside back, and then the seat. Other upholsterers, particularly in the United States, start by building up the seat deck and fully upholstering the pad before making a start on upholstering either the arms or the back. The blueprint methods on pages 224–249 set out suggested orders of work for different types of chair, which you can adapt to suit your own needs.

Remembering to break each project down into manageable bite-sized areas is key to planning out the final stage. Each pad tends to have an area referred to as a "corridor" – the main focal point that your eye latches onto when you first look at the piece (see page 77). The pattern matching should be at its best along the corridors.

Measuring and cutting

If you haven't already done a cutting plan (see page 79), it's worth spending some time doing one now, before you cut out your top cover. By now, of course, you will have a clear understanding of the size and volume of each pad to be covered, which will make it easy to check over your measurements and make any changes to the cutting plan. Chapter 2 (pages 73–82) explains how to work out how much fabric you need, devise the most cost-effective cutting plan and mark the fabric panels; these are things that should be taken into consideration at the very beginning, even though you may not actually cut out and apply the top cover until you have completed all the stages of the upholstery process up to the muslin (calico) layer.

Checking fabric before you cut

As a general rule, fabric comes on the roll with the right side facing inward. When the fabric is unrolled, the bottom of the pattern will be at the cut edge of the roll. But always check that the fabric is the correct pattern and colour and is free of faults before you cut into the roll, so that you don't get a nasty shock later on. Most fabric suppliers will have a printed reminder tucked into the fabric to this effect.

Lots of my students find the idea of putting on the top cover very daunting, but everything you've done so far – from applying the burlap layer right through to the muslin (calico) – has been a kind of dress rehearsal for this final stage. The basic frame shape is still the same: nothing has moved and, although the pad is now thicker than it was when you first began, all the cuts that you make in the top fabric are by and large the same as those you've already made in previous fabric layers. This is the exciting part – the bit you've been looking forward to ever since you first decided to take up the project!

I find it is key to not get bogged down in the nuances of the shape you're working on. Regardless of the size, shape or even the role of any particular pad, the basic processes that you will have gone through on each pad are similar enough to allow a consistent approach to fitting the top covers.

Setting on

Let's start with plain fabric. With plain fabrics such as linen, which have a looser and more obvious weave than something like a satin, you can see the warp and weft very clearly – and therefore position the fabric pieces along the key "corridors" (see page 77) more easily – without the distraction of pattern over the top. Provided you make sure that the warp and weft are square along the main corridors, the eye can easily forgive any slight distortions in the weave around the edges of the pad, where perhaps the fabric stretches on the bias.

With patterned fabrics, when you marked out and cut the different pieces, you should already have aligned the warp direction up and down each piece and the weft from side to side, taking the pattern placements and any pattern repeat into account. But remember: don't allow yourself to be distracted by the pattern too much at this stage; you've already made decisions about where the corridors fall on each piece at the cutting-plan stage, so now focus on the weave of the cloth and setting it on square.

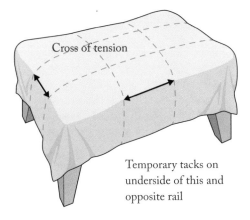

Cross of tension

Temporary tacks on underside of this and opposite rail

Temporary tacks on underside of this and opposite rail

1 As when setting on the burlap (see page 131), two or three well-placed temporary tacks forming the initial cross of tension will suffice. I suggest using ⅜" (10-mm) fine tacks rather than improved, partly to avoid hitting them into heavier tacks underneath and partly to avoid damaging the weave in case you need to re-position the fabric later on.

2 As when setting on the muslin (calico) (see page 181), place your hands a few inches apart on the fabric at the junction of the cross and gently push them together: if there's some excess fabric in between, your tension is too loose. Remove the tacks at both ends of the fabric, increase the tension and then re-tack. Do this in both directions on the cross of the fabric.

Temporary tacking

Most of the upholsterers I work with, young and old, temporary tack the top cover in place on all sides of the pad before they commit to fixing it off permanently, even if they're using a staple gun. This may feel like a waste of time to a beginner, but it avoids the trauma and expense of having to remove permanent tacks or staples, thus potentially damaging expensive fabric, if your initial tension is wrong.

Square, rectangular and evenly tapered pads

1. Using your initial cross of tension as a guide, expand the width of the cross by adding an extra tack either side of the three already inserted in any rail, and then go to the rail opposite that one and repeat the process.

2. Repeat step 1 on the two remaining rails.

3. Use a single tack on each corner to fix off and work a nice even stretch on the bias.

4. Gradually move outwards from the center of the rails, tacking opposite pairs of rails in turn, as in steps 1 and 2, until you either reach a corner or find the fabric restricted by a rail (see pages 133–140 for cuts).

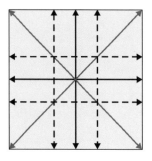

Square pad

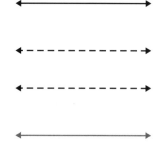

Rectangular pad

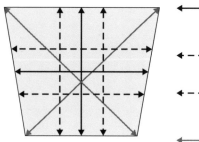

Evenly tapered pad

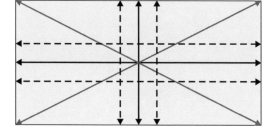

First set of three temporary tacks, centered on all four rails

Second and third sets of temporary tacks, expanding the cross of tension

Temporary tacks on the bias to fix the corners

Round and oval pads

1 Form your initial cross of tension at the quarter points on the circle, like hands on a clock – at 12:00 and then at the opposite point (6:00), then at 3:00, and 9:00. Then sub-divide it into eighths by placing your next temporary tacks halfway between two points (say at 1:30) and then opposite (7:30), and finally 10:30 and 4:30.

2 Divide the circle or oval up again into sixteenths, again tacking opposite sides in turn – 12:45–6:45; 11:15–5:15; 2:15–8:15; 3:45–9:45.

3 Keep subdividing in this way as necessary; the larger the diameter of the pad, the greater the number of divisions you will need.

It is absolutely essential to do this so as to maintain an even tension and avoid the weave slewing to one side.

Apply any cuts where necessary around legs following the methods described earlier, once again remembering to stop a little short of the rails that you are cutting around, as with the scrim and the muslin (calico) stages. Don't forget that you can always practice your cuts by using scraps of fabric as a "dry run."

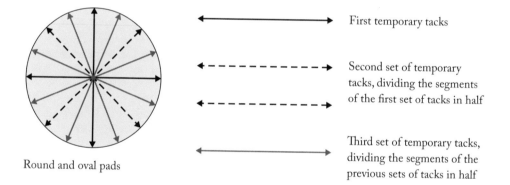

Round and oval pads

First temporary tacks

Second set of temporary tacks, dividing the segments of the first set of tacks in half

Third set of temporary tacks, dividing the segments of the previous sets of tacks in half

Tacking off

Tacking off is simply the process of hitting the temporary tacks all the way in and fixing the top cover in place. Do this once you are sure the tension and pattern alignment are correct. There are a few caveats, however:

☐ If you're using a patterned fabric, it's often useful to leave the temporary tacks in place until every panel has been tacked. That way you can check the pattern alignment once all the fabric panels are in place.

☐ If you're doing multiple chairs that need to look identical – for example, a set of dining chairs – temporary tack the covers in place on all the chairs, rather than dealing with each one individually.

☐ If the edges of the pad look slightly corrugated or crinkled, it might be that the tacks have been placed too far apart. It's worth inserting additional temporary tacks in between those already there, remembering to re-apply some tension in the cloth before you do so.

☐ Make sure the tacks are driven well into the frame.

☐ If you find that some tacks are bouncing out or cannot grip all the layers of fabric, consider increasing the tack size – but stick with fine rather than improved tacks.

Covering scrolled pads

Fitting a cover on a scrolled arm or back requires special consideration, as you need to work the cover around the pad's seemingly complex curves. This is where the fabric's inherent stretch on the bias will come into its own and aid the tight and smooth fitting of a cover. Scrolls are an extension of the effect that the crown of a pad has. Some of the processes are a little different in regard to how you achieve each step, but the order of work for both construction and covering is the same for scrolled pads as for standard pads.

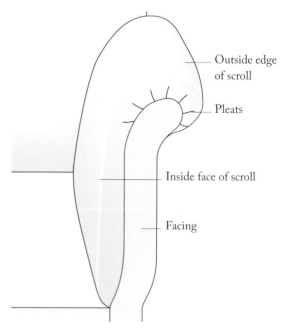

Outside edge of scroll

Pleats

Inside face of scroll

Facing

Areas of a scrolled pad.

Pattern placement on scroll rolls

Finding the best place to center the focal element of a pattern on a scroll can be a little tricky. Choosing the measured mid-point of a panel is rarely the only consideration. In addition to centering the pattern on the piece of fabric, you also have to think about how much of the panel will actually be visible when all the upholstering is complete. For example, if you're upholstering a scrolled back, then you want the main motif(s) of the pattern to be situated halfway up the inside back, so that it's visually pleasing as you look at the chair. However, the scroll continues over to the outside back – so if you simply measure the total length of the scroll and position the main pattern motif at the halfway point, more often than not it will actually be too far up the scroll.

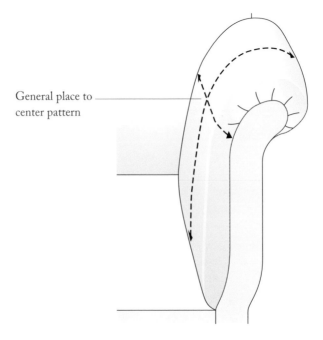

General place to center pattern

So think about the areas that will be visible and base your pattern placement on that, taking into account things like how high any adjoining pads (seat pads, for example) will be. A simple rule of thumb is that if the seat is a fixed or fully upholstered seat, then the center of the pattern on a scroll arm will typically need to be located below the measured center of the scroll panel. If the seat is a cushioned seat, however, then the center of the pad is more likely to marry with the center of the scroll panel. Remember that you will need to allow extra fabric to wrap around the scroll at the top and to pull through to the bottom to tack off on the lower rail. If you are intending to attach a fly (see page 197) to this panel, then that, of course, must be factored in, too.

When measuring the circumference of your pad to work out how much fabric you need, make sure you lay a fabric tape measure on the pad and poke it through the gap between the seat, back or arm to gauge where the tacking-off point will be; then (if fabric quantity allows) add a few inches extra to be on the safe side.

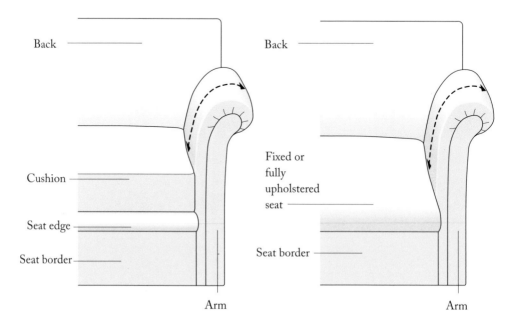

The addition of a cushioned seat reduces the visible inside face of the scroll.

Fly

If fabric quantity is tight or it is expensive, it's good practice to machine sew a strip of lining material or muslin (calico) to the base of the panel and use this to tack off onto the frame. This strip of fabric is called a fly and should not be so big that it can be seen once the panel is fitted in place.

Pleating on the edge of a scrolled pad

When fitting fabric around the leading edge of a scrolled pad, it can be tricky to cope with the excess fabric. Whether the pleats are tiny little gathers or formal folds in the cloth, it is very important to make them appear to radiate from one central focal point, which may be either in the center of the scroll on tightly curved scrolls or, like an artist's vanishing point, an implied center that lies somewhere off the actual piece, which suits more elliptical scrolls. The pleats should be used to enhance the natural curve of the scroll.

Creating a focal point on the edge of the scroll.

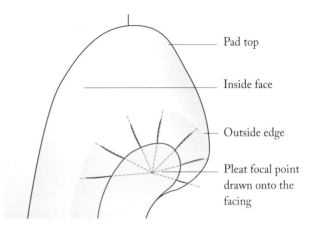

Pad top

Inside face

Outside edge

Pleat focal point drawn onto the facing

Most upholsterers would agree that pleats should be dressed so that the folds in the fabric are smoothest when your hand lightly rubs over them from the outside of the scroll inwards. How do individual upholsterers achieve this? I have my own preferences and I think that matching the spacing between pleats needs to be as consistent as possible and the pleat lengths should be equal. The basic rule is to avoid having obvious pleats facing upward, because they can trap dust and dirt easily. If the tension on the fabric is correct, that should give you a starting point for where your first pleat will naturally form.

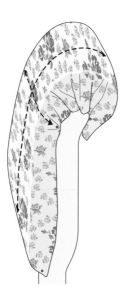

Leading edge of the pad

Pulling point

Pulling point

1 Follow the method for basic setting on (see applying burlap on page 131), but move the side-to-side center line up to just before the scroll forms. Ensure that the top, bottom, inside and outside edges are more securely temporary tacked, but temporary tack the fabric less frequently on the edges of the pad facings.

2 Around the leading edge of the scroll fabric, apply extra tension by stretching the top and bottom of the fabric at the same time. (It's not a disaster if you lose the tension when you tack one end: once those tacks are in position, you can re-tension the other end of the fabric.)

Professional tip

Your pleat should only really show on the facing with just a tiny amount visible on the leading edge, where the inside panel turns into the facing. If you allow the pleat to creep back onto the inside panel, it will catch and wear prematurely.

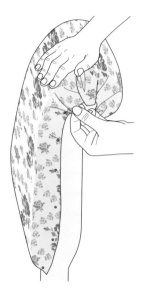

3 Dress the fabric over onto the front facing at the bottom of the scroll with your non-working hand and insert a few temporary tacks into the facing to hold the fabric in place.

4 Still working on the facing only, use your non-working hand to pull the fullness in the fabric upward, stretching it against the temporary tacks at the base. The fabric will naturally start to kink at the point where the circular shape of the scroll begins. You can use this kink as the basis of where the first pleat will form.

5 Turn that kink into a pleat by folding the fabric from the outside of the scroll toward the inside. The center of the circle or focal point (see page 197) should give you the natural angle that this pleat should follow, rather like the lines on a clock face. (If it helps, use a clean regulator or wooden pleating tool to help fold the fabric over.) Temporary tack it in place.

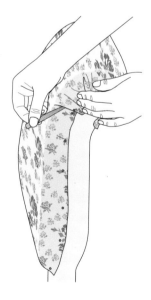

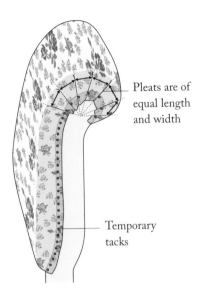

Pleats are of equal length and width

Temporary tacks

6 Once the first pleat is formed, it's a good idea to check that you have subdivided the remaining circumference of the facing into equal amounts to ensure that subsequent pleats are evenly spaced; again make sure that the pleats don't creep past and off the leading edge of the scroll and show on the inside face of the pad.

7 Once you've decided how many pleats you need, repeat steps 4 and 5 to form the remaining pleats. When you're happy with their positions, hit the tacks home.

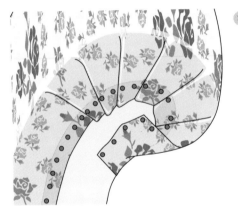

8 Occasionally, the last pleat will not radiate from the focal point. This usually occurs on wider scrolls and the final pleat often needs to cross over one or two of the previous pleats to enable it to make a clean fold. This is not unusual and actually helps to visually close off the end of the scroll.

Professional tip

If you're working on something that has two arms or faces to the scroll (for example, a nursing chair), you have to decide which side to start working on first. If you're right-handed, it's generally better work on the right-hand arm first. Your natural instinct might be to work on the left-hand side first, simply because it's slightly easier to maneuver your body and reach across the arm pad using your dominant hand. It's always going to be hard to match pleats and spacings on the second arm to those on the first, but if you've worked on your "unnatural" side first, you've got a much better chance of replicating them on your dominant side when you come to cover the second arm.

Seat platforms

The generic term "platform" is given to the layer of lining fabric used to cover areas of pads that will not be seen under cushions. Essentially, a platform is a large fly attached to a much smaller piece of top cover. Making a fly can save on limited or valuable fabric without compromising the overall look of the finished chair. If your chair seat can be seen from either side – for example, under the arm or from the back – then it is most likely that a platform would not be suitable.

If your chair has tension springs, it will most likely have a hemmed flap of platform lining laying over the springs to protect the cushion above. More valuable chairs have a quilted version that is often attached to the frame by elastic to allow it to flex, as the springs bend in the middle when the seat is sat on (see suspension systems).

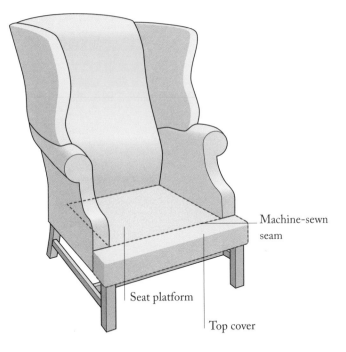

Area of seat platform.

Machine-sewn seam

Seat platform

Top cover

Quilted platform

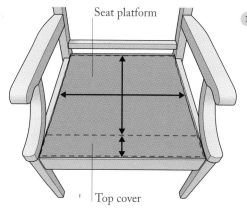

Seat platform

Top cover

1 Measure out the total area you need to cover both the seat platform and top cover (if you have not done this already). In addition, tension spring fixings at the sides of the seat will need to be covered if they are not already covered by a flap of webbing. Make sure the completed platform will be long enough to fix off on the front seat rail and to reach the back of the seat. For the seat platform, add a seam allowance of ½" (12 mm) to the sides, front and back measurements, and cut out two pieces of lining fabric to this size.

2 Pin the lining fabric pieces right sides together so that they don't slip, and machine sew the side and back edges only, leaving the front open to make a bag. Turn the bag right side out and, with your hand inside the bag, dress the seams so that they lie flat. You can press the seam flat if you wish, but avoid steam ironing the fabric, as steam can cause the salt in the dye to show as a tidemark on your platform.

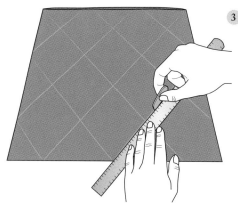

3 Using blackboard chalk, lightly mark out a diamond pattern on one side of your bag, bearing in mind that the smaller the diamonds are, the more machine sewing you will have to do. Diamonds around the size of your hand are fine.

4 Cut a piece of polyester batting the same size as your seat platform, insert it into the bag and once again dress the edges with your hand to make sure that both the polyester and the seams are flat. Now pin along the chalk lines so that each pin catches the batting between the two layers of lining cloth.

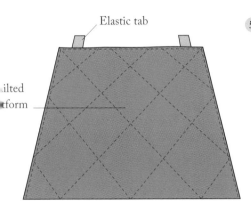

Elastic tab

ilted
form

5 Starting at the back, machine sew along the pinned lines. Sew all of the diagonal lines in one direction first and then switch to sewing the second direction to form the quilted diamonds. Now top stitch around the side and back edges of the quilted platform. Sew two or three folded lengths of elastic tape to the back edge for fixing it onto the frame.

6 Cut out two strips of top-cover fabric, remembering to add a ½" (12-mm) seam allowance along the side and back edges plus enough to allow you to turn over and tack off on the front rail along the front edge of the chair frame.

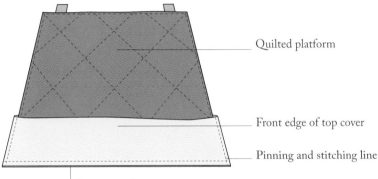

Quilted platform

Front edge of top cover

Pinning and stitching line

Open raw edges

7 Lay the pieces of top-cover fabric right sides together and pin them down the sides. Sew down the sides and take out the pins. With right sides still together, slip the top-cover "bag" over your quilted platform. Pin and stitch together ½" (12 mm) in from the raw open edge, making sure that the seams at the sides of the top cover are aligned with the sides of the quilted platform.

8 Turn the top-cover section right side out so that the seam joining it to the quilted lining pad is hidden inside the cover, and use your hand to dress the seams flat inside. This pocket can be filled with a variety of layers of battings, but in general a layer of cotton felt sandwiched in between layers of polyester batting should suffice.

Fitting a quilted platform

Platforms are rarely fixed side to side when covering tension springs. This lack of side fixing and the elastic attachment on the back of the platform are what allow it to flex downward and not rear away from the frame when the seat is sat on.

1 Lay the platform on top of the tension springs, so that the platform either touches the inside back or is flush with the back rail. Work out how much fabric will be needed to fold under and fix off on the front edge. Next, attach the elastic to the back rail with a couple of staples or tacks.

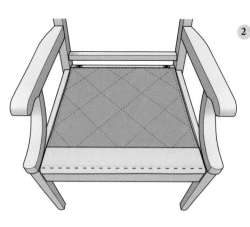

2 Neatly staple or tack the front of the platform to the top of the seat rail, taking care to apply a little tension to the cover – but not so much that you compress the springs. Trim off the excess at the front, leaving enough fabric to turn back on itself and tack off. There are numerous ways of fixing the front of the platform onto the rail, so be led by how the original was fitted.

Wings

Like scrolled pads, wings often require a few pleats to bend the fabric around the tighter curve found at the front of the wing at the top. These pleats are easier to apply to wings, as they are often very short pleats with only about ¾" (2 cm) or so of the fabric showing once the fabric is fitted. Typically, two simple Y-cuts will be needed to enable a tight-fitting cover – one where the wing meets the arm top and one to fit the cover around the top of the back rail. When placing a pattern on a wing, make sure it is aligned to the pattern on adjacent pads and therefore looks part of the pattern as a whole and not an afterthought.

Fitting the cover with a good pull around the leading edge is, as always, the key to removing fullness. Because of the tension, fewer and smaller pleats are required to fit around the rounded corners. Make sure the warp and the weft are as square to the frame as possible throughout; balancing perfect tension in the cover with a square weave as the fabric wraps around the wing is vital.

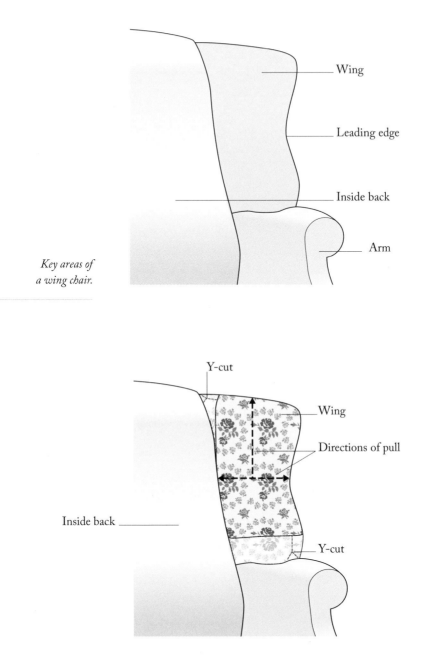

*Key areas of
a wing chair.*

Wing

Leading edge

Inside back

Arm

Y-cut

Wing

Directions of pull

Inside back

Y-cut

Setting on a wing cover

1 Temporary tack the cover to the rails either side of the pad across the center and in the center of the top rail. Make the Y-cuts that allow the cover to pull around the rails at the top of the arm and at the top of the wing where the wing meets the back rail, but do not tack them off just yet.

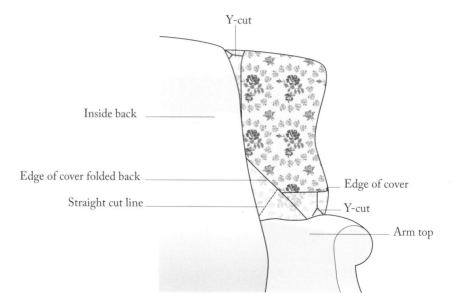

Y-cut

Inside back

Edge of cover folded back

Straight cut line

Edge of cover

Y-cut

Arm top

2 Apply a single straight cut where the back of the wing meets the top of the arm; this prevents the fabric from rucking up when the cover pulls through the gap between the top of the arm and the bottom of the wing. Once cut, tuck the excess fabric through the gap and temporary tack it to the top of the arm.

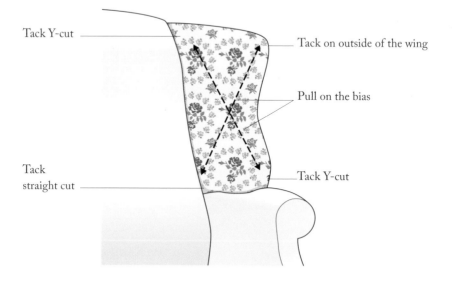

Tack Y-cut

Tack on outside of the wing

Pull on the bias

Tack straight cut

Tack Y-cut

3 Now pull the cover on the bias in both directions and temporary tack the Y-cuts, then the straight cut and finally the outside of the wing.

Fixing the cover

Once the tension has been fixed into the cover, forming the pleats is very simple. Just as with scrolled pads, start with the bottom of the leading edge (where the front of the wing meets the top of the arm) and pull up and out lightly from this point, temporary tacking the fabric to the rails as you move along. As with a scroll, the first pleat on a wing will form naturally as you work around the edge. Don't forget to tack the opposite rail as you go to prevent the fabric from slewing to one side.

Once the first pleat has been set, follow the same method as for scrolled pads and check the pleats will be even in width and length. Once you are happy with their position, temporary tack them. Continue to temporary tack along the top edge of the wing, matching the pull and tacks at the bottom of the wing. Once you are happy with the fit, permanently tack off the cover with ⅜" (10-mm) fine tacks or staple the cover off.

Piping

Piping is generally best cut on the bias, as it's less likely to ruck and crinkle as it goes round a curve, although it can be cut along either the warp or the weft of the fabric.

The ideal width of each piping strip is 1½" (4 cm). This will result in a seam allowance that is equal to the seam allowance typically used for upholstery machine stitching of around ½" (12 mm). Thicker or thinner piping cords than the standard no. 3 may need different allowances.

Making piping

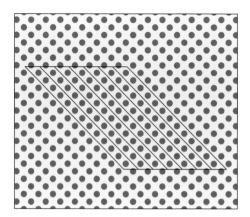

1 Chalk your lines on the face of the fabric at 1½" (4-cm) intervals, making sure that they're at 45 degrees to the straight grain. Cut out around the edge of your marked-out panel of bias strips.

2 Fold over the top edge toward you and chalk a line on the reverse of the fabric, all the way across. This line represents the top of the fabric. When the strips have been cut, you will know which end of each strip is the top.

3 Cut along the 45-degree lines drawn in step 1.

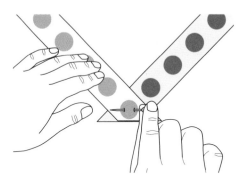

4 If necessary, join strips together to make a long enough length. Lay two pieces right sides together at right angles, and pin together so that the pin goes across the intersection of the two strips.

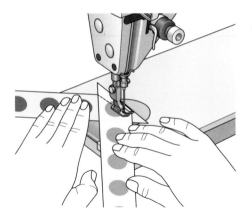

5 Sew along the intersection, following the direction of the pin – but remove the pin so that you don't sew over it. Press the seam open. Attach more strips in this way until you have the total length that you need.

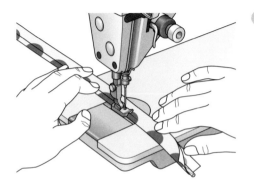

6 Fold the strip in half, with wrong sides together, sandwiching the piping cord in the middle. Machine stitch along the length, stitching close to the piping cord. If you have a piping foot for your machine, it will make this process much easier. If not, you can use a zipper foot. It's very difficult to do with a standard machine foot, as you cannot stitch close enough to the piping cord.

Borders and facings

Once fabrics for the main panel or panels (seat, arms, back, and wings) have been fitted, usually the next process is to fit any borders and facings. The most common place to find a border is on the front of the seat. The most common place to find facings is at the front of arms, but they can be a part of backs, too. The main advantage of using a border or facing is to hide the frilly edge of a panel that forms after tacking the fabric to a wooden rail. (Imagine the top of a cola bottle – it's a flat disk of metal clamped over the top, forming a wavy edge. The same kind of wavy edge occurs on almost every deep pad, because the fabric has been stretched over the crown of the pad.) The simplest way of masking this frill is to stitch a panel of fabric over it.

Most borders or facings are simply strips of fabric cut across the roll that are then either fixed directly onto the frame or hand sewn onto the upholstery. Generally, it's advisable to either self-pipe the fabric or to mask the join with pre-made cord (see page 215).

Cutting and positioning the border or facing

1. Start by measuring the area you need to cover. Add 2" (5 cm) to each end and the bottom edge for fixing onto the frame. If you're adding piping, add an extra ½" (12 mm) for the seam allowance. For details of how to make piping, see page 207.

2. Chalk a line directly onto the pad where you're applying the border or facing. Use blackboard chalk rather than tailor's chalk as it's easier to blow off. This line should be the line that the top of your border rests against to give you a smooth and consistent finish.

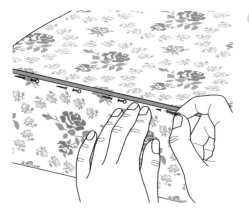

3. Pin the border in place, right side facing out, following your previous chalk line, spacing the pins about 1½" (4 cm) apart and adjusting the pattern alignment if necessary. If the border is piped, insert your pins along the machine line, holding the piping cord in place. Don't worry: provided you've used appropriately sized pins, you won't damage the stitch line between the piping and the main border fabric.

4 Flip the fabric over the top of the pins, so that the reverse side of the border is showing. Lightly pin the border up and out of the way. Assess how much stuffing is going to be required in the border. I tend to use layered battings for borders, as the thickness and density are consistent throughout. It's worth noting that the volume of stuffing in the border will compress significantly when the border is pulled tight and tacked off.

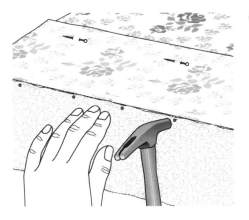

5 Using very few tacks, permanently tack the batting to the frame to avoid the batting rucking up when the cover is pulled tight. If there's no frame to tack to, use a very light tacking stitch using a curved slipping needle and a thin cotton thread.

6 Remove the pins holding the border out of the way. Temporary tack the border cover down in place. Avoid putting too much tension in at this stage, as you may simply pull the pins out from the pad.

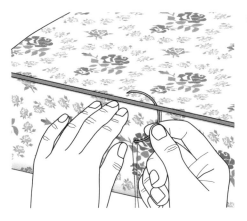

7 Slipstitch (see page 214) the border in place along the chalked line, making sure the stitch length is no more than ⅜" (1 cm).

8 You can now remove the temporary tacks along the edge opposite the hand-sewn edge and permanently tack as you go, using fine tacks and ensuring that the pattern alignment is maintained.

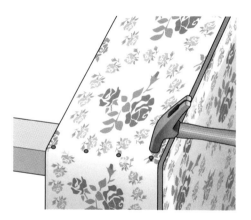

9 Stretch the border from end to end and permanently tack it in place.

Back-tacked borders

Back-tacking strip is a simple strip of strong cardboard ⅜" (1 cm) wide that can be tacked or stapled through without weakening it. When tacked over a flap of fabric, the fabric can then be folded back against the cardboard edge (which won't buckle) to give the appearance of a hand-sewn finish. Back tacking a border against piping can save time and is a more commercially practiced technique for finishing off the border.

1 Fix your piping to the frame with tacks or staples.

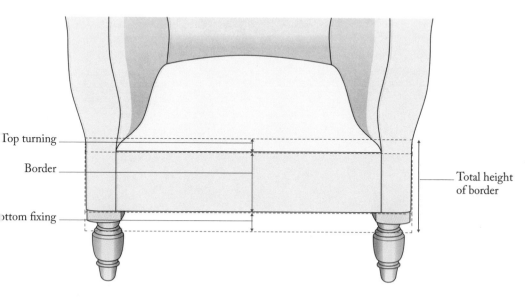

Top turning

Border

ʒottom fixing

Total height of border

2 Measure and cut your strip of border material, adding a ⅝" (1.5-cm) turning at the top of the border plus an amount to pull and tack off underneath.

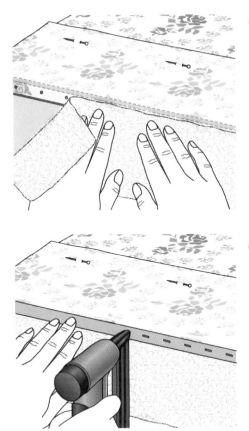

3 Lay the border fabric face down against the piping and upside down so that the raw edge of your border panel lines up with the cut edge of the piping. Tack or staple them together ⅝" (1.5 cm) from the raw edge. Cut a piece of polyester batting exactly the same size as the border panel and lay it over the top.

4 Position the back-tacking cardboard as close as possible to the piping cord and staple through all of the layers so that the cardboard has clamped everything tight to the piping line. Flip the border fabric back on itself and tack it off on the underside of the chair.

Hand-sewn facing

A facing is a panel of fabric on the front of an arm or the side of a back. Hand sewing facings is a great way of ensuring that the detail and shape of a facing is at its best. There are more production-based ways of fitting them, but for the vast majority of chairs I tend to prefer the hand-sewn option.

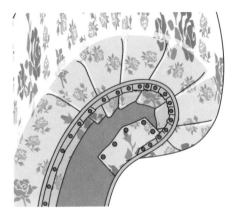

1 Tack your piping to the wooden frame, ensuring that the piping follows the chalk line as it will form the outline of the facing panel. Turn the ends of the piping back in on themselves so that they don't fray.

2 Add padding to the facing by tacking batting onto the frame, finishing just shy of the piping. Put in enough padding to prevent you from feeling the lumps and bumps of the rails and the upholstery fixed onto them – but don't be too generous or you may end up with bulky, dome-shaped facings.

3 Pin the facing in place with upholstery pins. Make sure that the folded edge of the fabric is as smooth as possible where it butts up to the piping. It's important to have a reasonable amount of tension between the pins, as once the facing has been sewn in place it will be difficult to add more tension without re-sewing.

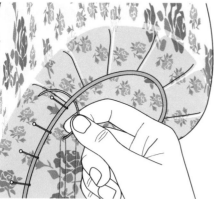

4 Slipstitch the facing in place, making sure that you sew through all the layers with each stitch, and that you keep your stitch length around ⅜" (1 cm) long to avoid the fabric having a kinked appearance where the stitches pull tight. Then tack the final remaining open end down onto the frame.

Slipstitches

Slipstitches are the main way that upholsterers close off panels with invisible stitching when a tack or a staple won't do. Waxed slipping thread is hard to snap by hand so is durable, and its waxed coating allows it to slide easily through the strong weave structure of most top covers. The traditional slipstitch has a couple of vernacular names that pretty much describe the basic pattern of the stitches—these are castle stitch or ladder stitch.

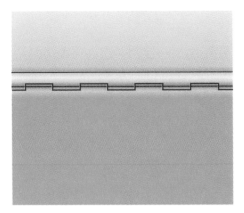

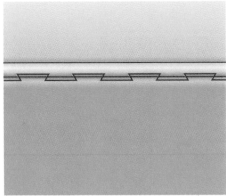

Castle or ladder stitch

The shape formed by the thread is reminiscent of the top of a castle wall – hence the stitch's most common name of castle stitch. This shape of stitch is suited to very stable fabrics that do not have much in the way of inherent stretch, generally made from 100% natural fibers such as pure silk. This stitch represents the older style of slipstitching.

Dovetail-style slipstitch

Since the invention of modern manmade fibers and the refinement of traditional weaving techniques, fabrics have tended to become a little stretchier. This has led to a variant of the traditional castle stitch, in which the splayed shape of the stitch is more reminiscent of a dovetail pattern.

Dovetail-style slipstitch with piping

As the most common slipstitch used today isn't a true castle stitch, we will look at the dovetail-style stitch in more detail. Typically, piping is used as a way of masking the join between the two main panels being slipstitched together. Use a slipping thread closest to the main color of your fabric. If you are not able to do this, choose something darker than your top cover as the finished stitches are usually in shadow. The new stitches should, of course, never show, but with time, the pad edge will soften, which can lead to hand-stitched seams opening a fraction. Ensure that the border or facing is well pinned in place and make sure that the padding/batting isn't rucked up under the cover along the general line you will follow with the stitches.

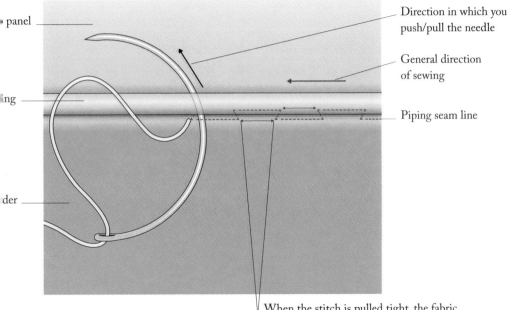

panel

ng

der

Direction in which you push/pull the needle

General direction of sewing

Piping seam line

When the stitch is pulled tight, the fabric is slightly stretched at these points, which helps to hide the thread.

1 Thread a slipping needle (a 2½" (6-cm), 20-gauge curved slipping needle is ideal for most slipping duties) with a length of waxed slipping thread no longer than the span of your arms outstretched. Knot off one end of the thread using two or three half-hitches, in the same way as you would when sewing a button onto a shirt.

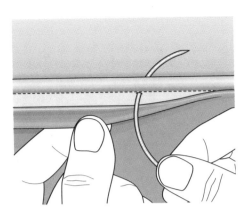

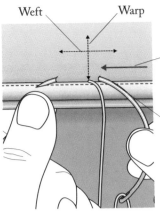

Weft Warp

Direction of stitch

Insert the needle a few strands back from where it came out

2 With your non-working hand, bend the border back slightly so that you expose the machine thread line on the piping. Insert the needle into the piping just below the machine line (which will help to hide the knot when the stitches are pulled tight). Pull the needle and the thread all the way through so that the knot is pulled tight against the piping.

3 Now carefully peel the piping back slightly so that you can see the slipping thread exiting the back of the piping. Assuming that your direction of sewing is from right to left, count a few strands of weave to the right of the slipping thread's exit hole and push the needle into the top cover, ensuring that the curved needle can travel easily to the left. Bring the needle out about ⅜" (1 cm) further along, draw the needle all the way out and pull the thread lightly so as to not overtighten.

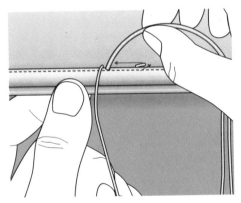

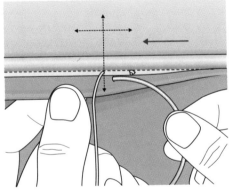

4 Now the needle must be pushed back through to the front of the piping. Line the needle up with the exit hole from the last stitch, insert it into the piping just outside (or above) the machine line and draw both the needle and thread all the way out.

5 Once again, count a few strands of weave back to the right of the exit hole in the piping, insert the needle into the border/facing cover and bring it out about ⅜" (1 cm) further along. Try not to catch up the stuffings as you draw the needle along, and try to have the thread sit just below the surface of the border cloth.

6 Take the needle back through the piping directly adjacent to the exit hole from the last stitch. Count a few strands of weave back to the right and insert the needle into the cover aiming for an exit ⅜" (1 cm) to the left. Draw the last full stitch tight and continue to sew along the length of the border or around the panel being fitted.

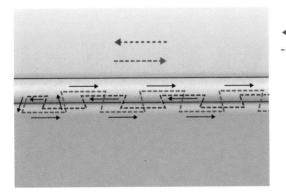

◀ - - - - - - -   Forward stitching direction
- - - - - - - ▶   Reverse stitching direction

7 To cast off a row of slipstitches, sew back in the opposite direction for three or four stitches. It's best to offset your reverse stitches so that they pull halfway along your previous stitches, as this avoids widening the stitch holes made in the top cover. Snip the end of the thread as close to the cover as possible and it should pop inside the cover with a light rub with your thumb.

Professional tips

☐ Keep your fingers dry and clean. Gripping a slipping needle can be fiddly and any body oils mixed with general upholstery dust can easily stain a fabric. Rubber needle pulls are widely available from haberdashers and are effective.

☐ Tempting as it may be to lengthen your stitches as you go, avoid the temptation as most stitches will be seen as tiny pulls in the surface of the cloth and, while the eye tends to forgive these tiny pulls if they are evenly spaced, they can look messy if they are not.

☐ When slipstitching panels together without piping, you will need to take more care to ensure that the slipping thread is not visible when the stitch is pulled tight and to maintain an even tension throughout your stitches.

☐ Pre-machine sewing the piping to the border or one edge of a panel of fabric is also required from time to time. In most cases, this means that the slipping thread need not be pulled through the piping and into the border. Because the border is already sewn to the piping, you can just catch up the inside edge of the piping and sew that to the main panel.

Outside panels and undersides

Closing the outsides of chairs can often be a challenge, even though it involves less work in terms of adding fillings and battings. It is tempting to rush this stage, but you need to pay particular attention to pattern placement (see page 77) to ensure alignment with the inside panels.

These outside panels are most commonly referred to as outside wings, outside arms and outside backs – abbreviated as OW, OA and OB. They involve fewer steps to complete, but slimmer pads are more prone to showing lumps and bumps from earlier processes. Revisiting one or two rushed or not fully resolved areas of tacking off left over from fixing the inside panels can be time well spent.

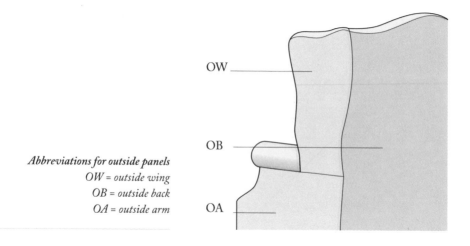

Abbreviations for outside panels
OW = outside wing
OB = outside back
OA = outside arm

Closing outside panels edged by single piping

The typical order of work for this stage is: fit piping to the OW edges, apply linings, fit batting layer or layers, and cut and pin the cover in place. The most common way of closing the outside panels is to hand sew them in place using a slipstitch (see page 214). Once the OW covers are secure, then move on to the OAs and then the OB.

Where the piping is placed can have an effect on how generous the pads look as a whole, so try to strike a balance between following the lines and curves in the frame while retaining the fullness of the inside pad. If the frame and upholstery turn a sharp 90 degrees, then any piping framing the outside panel should do so, too. Understanding this simple relationship between the placement of the piping and the overall appearance will develop with experience. Before you do the outsides, pin the piping in place on the edge of the frame, as this will allow you to assess the proportions and fullness.

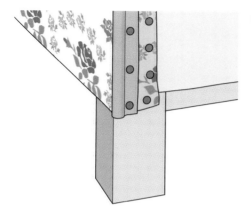

1. Once you're happy with the position of the piping, tack it in place, ensuring that the raw edge is firmly fixed into place with a reasonably close tack or staple placement. One tack every 1" (2.5 cm) should be suitable; staples can be placed closer together because they occupy less space, but make sure you are happy with the placement before you fix them permanently.

2. Trim off the excess fabric left over from fixing off the internal panels. All of the fabric tacked onto the frame that falls inside the piping line is also held into place by the staples or tacks holding the piping, so in theory all of the excess can be removed before you line the outsides and fit the batting. Be careful not to trim anything off that is vital or undo any tacks that are key to holding the inside panel fabric tight.

Lining the outside panels

Lining the outside panels is the next process. The lining spans the frame and gives support to the outside battings and cover; it can also help to form the curves and give a suggestion of fullness to the outsides, while allowing the upholstery to remain thin. With this in mind, I tend to prefer using muslin (calico) to line the frame, as it is less bulky than the traditional option of burlap or off-cuts of fabric from a previous job.

1. Measure the size of the panel without being too generous—you shouldn't need too much fabric, as the edges of the panel do not need turning if the lining fabric is sufficiently tightly woven.

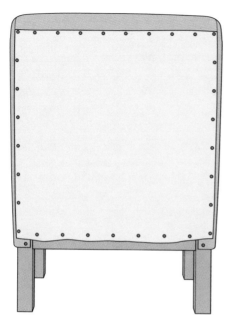

2 Set the lining fabric in place, creating the central cross of tension (see page 131). Then tack off the bias points and fill in between. Try to tack off a good 1¼–1½" (3–4 cm) in from the edge of the rails or piping, and make sure that all tacks or staples are hit home firmly so that they won't be felt through the top cover.

3 Trim off the excess lining fabric so that it can't ruck up under the top cover. Remember to not fold the edges and re-tack, as this will only add bulk to the outside of the panel and will need additional padding to mask the fold.

Applying batting to the outside panels

Applying the batting will vary depending on which type of batting is to be used. Cotton felt is too bulky to be useful for all applications, but it comes into its own if there are excessive bumps created by the fitting of the inside panels, or if the frame edges are not clean enough to be softened by polyester batting alone. Due to its cost, skin batting is rarely used these days for lining outsides.

1 Choose the appropriate batting material and cut or tear off a piece that is just a fraction larger than the area to be filled. Try to hold the batting in place with as few fixings as possible. Usually the batting will move slightly when the cover is pulled tight, so too many fixings will potentially restrict this and form a ruck or lump when the cover is fitted.

2 Simply trim off the excess batting apart from the bottom edges, where it's good to fix the polyester layer of batting off on the underside of the chair.

Fitting the outside panel fabric

However you choose to secure the outside fabric, be it with slipstitching or tacking with decorative nails, the basic method will remain the same.

1 Measure, mark out and cut your top cover if you have not yet done so.

2 Following the sequence described at the start of this section (starting with outside wings if your chair has them, then outside arms and finally outside back), set your first panel in place with temporary tacks in the same way as you have done for all layers so far.

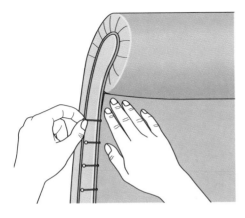
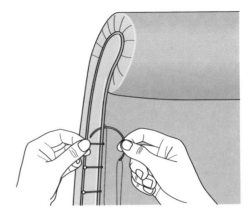

3 Pin your cover in place if you are hand sewing the outsides closed, or turn the edges under and tack off. If you intend to cover the edges with either decorative nails or braid, turn your edges under and tack off neatly.

4 Hand sew the edges of the panel that require it and tack off the rest before moving on to the next panel.

Back tacking outside arms

If your chair has a clearly defined rail on the underside of the arm that you are able to back tack the top of the outside arm to, you may be able to save time without compromising on quality. Follow the method for back-tacked borders (see page 211), because in essence that's all that an outside panel is. Turning the chair upside down will make it easier to see the rail that you will be back tacking along.

Decorative finishes

Decorative finishes are used to mask fixings around the edges of pads where slip stitching has not been possible or is not desirable. The two main forms are decorative nails which are driven into the frame with a hammer, or braid which is glued directly over the tacks or staples.

Decorative nails

Most traditional chairs tend to have decorative nails at the tops of the legs, covering the fabric where it can be tough to get the finish really crisp. This technique can be used around the edge of any panel provided that the wood is strong enough.

Decorative nails take a swift tap from your upholstery hammer to get them to bite into the wood and then a couple of weakly placed taps with the hammer to hit them home. There are hundreds of types of decorative nail to choose from, and a few are more suited to being glued into place – so check to make sure that you have chosen the right type.

Typically, decorative nails are attached so they butt up close to one another but they can also be evenly spaced with gaps inbetween.

Braid

Applying scroll gimp or straight braid can be a little trickier, as it requires the use of glue. The most commonly used type of glue is hot melt glue, but you can also use latex-based glue that can be brushed onto the back of the braid. Colored gimp pins (tiny painted pins available in a variety of colours) can be used in areas where the glue cannot form a bond or a corner is too tight to turn the braid unaided.

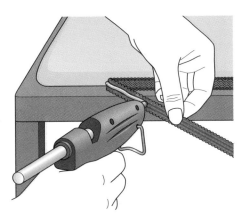

I advise gluing no more than a hand's span at a time, which will allow you time to work on getting the finish clean and accurate rather than fighting a long length of glued braid that you are attempting to keep from sticking to the wrong part of your chair.

Dust or bottoming cloth

Essentially, the dust or bottoming cloth is there to both hide the modesty of the fillings and to protect the floor under the chair from any debris or particles that build up as a chair is used. Fitting it is usually the last process in closing up the completed piece, and can be either a joy or a frustration. After you have spent quality time building comfortable inside panels and applying clean-fitting outside panels, the underside will most likely be the only part of the chair where the tacks are visible – but the quality and care that you take over tacking off this rarely seen part should be consistent with the rest of the chair, even though not on show.

Most bottoming cloths require just a few simple straight cuts to fit around the legs. On occasion, I like to use an extravagant off-cut from a previous project, which I fit to piece as a treat for anyone curious enough to turn the finished chair or stool over.

Use ⅜" (10-mm) fine tacks and keep your tack spacing to around 1" (2.5 cm), making sure that the tacks are hit home squarely. If you are fitting the dust cloth with staples, it's just as important to make sure that none has misfired or is poking out oddly.

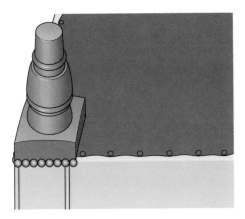

Blueprint methods

Chapter 6

Blueprint methods

These blueprints have been devised as a guide to show how similar techniques and materials can be applied to a wide variety of chair styles. They are listed in order of increasing levels of complexity.

Drop-in dining-chair seat pad

This style of pad has the simplest upholstery techniques and materials.

Sprung stuffover dining chair

This style of seat pad has structure from the springing and the traditional interpretation contains edge-stitching techniques.

Tub chair

This type of chair uses a combination of pad construction techniques, requires the arm/back pad to be curved, has more complicated issues around pattern alignment and adds additional features such as facings and outside panels.

Wing chair

This contains a combination of pinstuffed, stuffover and sprung stuffover pads and requires more extensive use of the techniques explored in the earlier chair styles.

Each style of chair has an order of work for both traditional upholstery and modern upholstery. Traditional upholstery uses natural fibers to create the shape and volume of the upholstered pads, while modern upholstery uses foam cut to the thickness required prior to upholstering, which speeds up the process significantly.

I don't feel its my place to dictate which style of filling (modern or traditional) is best for your projects, because only you will know your circumstances and areas of interest. There are, however, some points you should consider when choosing both your upholstery project and whether to go for a traditional or a modern filling.

First, assess your skill level and be honest with yourself. If you are a beginner, then you really should be looking at a drop-in seat pad as your starting point. Not only does the project contain the fewest steps, but they are shorter, too.

Using foam products can be much faster than traditional fillings, and still have a lifespan, but foam may not be the most appropriate material from a historical point of view – so if you are looking for a less time-consuming project, then look for a more modern chair to ensure that the fillings are authentic.

It is not always necessary to replace all of the fillings every time, so if you are looking for a quicker project, consider simply re-covering a piece where the upholstery is in good condition.

Start out by using inexpensive fabrics specifically woven for upholstery uses—at least until your confidence has grown: it only takes a misplaced snip of the shears or an over-enthusiastic tug in the wrong place to make the need for a second, or even a third, cover.

So take your time when choosing a project and balance your desire to progress with your skill level and the time you have available.

Don't be afraid to cherry pick segments of my techniques and work them into techniques that you may have learned either first hand or from other books. Try to use the blueprints as a guide and tick off the processes one by one. As you work backward during the ripping-out phase, most chairs reveal the secret of how they best go back together, so make sure that you take careful notes as you rip each chair down.

In this modern drop-on, the seat is attached to the sub frame of the chair using long wood screws, rather than sitting inside a frame.

Drop-in dining-chair seat pad

Traditional drop-in seat with simple pinstuffed pad

This style of pad typically has the simplest upholstery techniques and materials.

Rip down/strip out.

Mark out, position, and fix jute webbing to the frame, staying inside the frame markings.

Fix 12-oz (340-gram) burlap over the webbing.

Mark out and apply finger-tight stuffing ties.

Stuff with loose horsehair or coir.

Measure, cut out, and set on the muslin (calico), using temporary tacks.

Apply a layer of skin batting or cotton felt and then polyester batting.

Measure, cut out, and set on the top cover.

Tack down the sides and corners, forming pleats where required.

Measure, cut, and fit the bottom cloth.

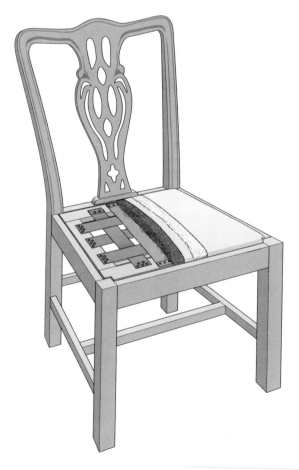

Traditional drop-in seat

Modern drop-in seat

A simple construction of foam and layered fillings (see foam chart on page 57).

Rip down/strip out.

Mark out, position and fix elasticated webbing to the frame, staying inside the frame markings.

Fix either 12-oz (340-gram) burlap or a synthetic equivalent over the webbing.

Mark out and cut a piece of seating-density foam.

Glue or staple the foam to the frame.

Measure, cut out, and fix polyester batting to the foam, using spray adhesive.

Measure, cut out, and set on the top cover.

Tack down the sides and corners, forming pleats where required.

Measure, cut, and fit the bottom cloth.

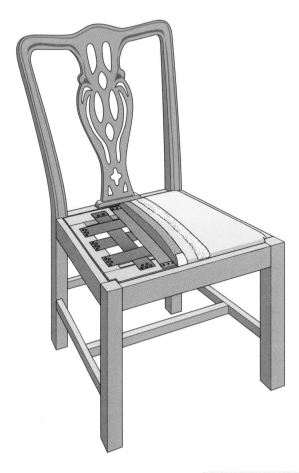

Modern drop-in seat

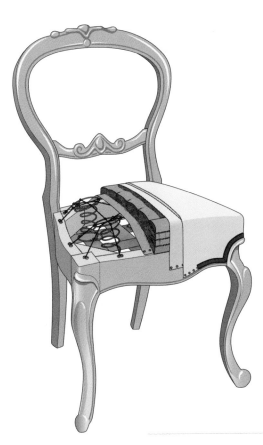

Traditional sprung stuffover seat

Sprung stuffover dining chair

Traditional sprung stuffover seat
Stuffover pad over sprung base, using loose horsehair or coir stuffing.
Rip down/strip out.
Mark out, position and fix the webbing to the frame, staying inside the frame markings.
Plan out the double-cone spring positions, ensuring even distribution, and secure the springs with spring ties.
Stabilize the springs by lashing them with laid cord.
Fix 12-oz (340-gram) burlap over the springs and apply a second set of spring ties to attach them to the burlap.
Mark out and apply the stuffing ties.
Stuff with loose horsehair or coir.
Set on linen scrim.
Secure the center of the pad with bridle ties and temporary tack the edges of the linen scrim.
Regulate the stuffings and add additional stuffing where required.
Tack off the linen scrim.

Mark out guidelines and make the blind stitches.

Mark out and apply top stitches to form the top roll.

Mark out and apply finger-tight stuffing ties for the second stuffing.

Stuff with a second stuffing of horsehair or coir.

Measure, cut out, and set on the muslin (calico), using temporary tacks.

Permanently tack the muslin (calico) in place.

Apply a layer of skin batting or cotton felt and then polyester batting.

Measure, cut out, and set on the top cover.

Permanently tack off the top cover.

Attach trimming where the edges of the pad meet the show wood, if required.

Measure, cut, and fit the bottom cloth.

In this deconstructed modern sprung stuffover seat, the rubberized webbing is attached directly to the frame. The foam elements of the seat have been enclosed in fabric and are in fact completely detached from the frame.

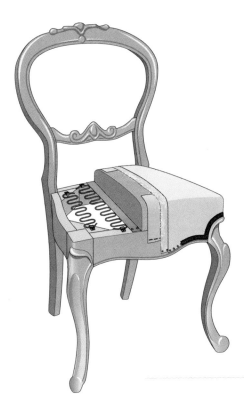

Modern sprung stuffover seat

Serpentine springs or elastic webbing, with foam and polyester filling.
Rip down/strip out.
Mark out, position, and fix either serpentine springs or elasticated webbing to the frame, staying inside the frame markings.
Stabilize the springs by lashing them with laid cord.
Fix either 12-oz (340-gram) burlap or a synthetic alternative over the springs.
Mark out and cut a piece of seating-density foam.
Glue or staple the foam directly to the frame or apply muslin (calico) strips to the foam and then staple them to the frame.
Measure, cut, and fix polyester batting to the foam, using spray adhesive.
Measure, cut out, and set on the top cover.
Permanently tack down the sides and corners, forming pleats where required.
Attach trimming where the edges of the pad meet the show wood if required.
Measure, cut, and fit the bottom cloth.

Tub chair

Traditional tub chair

A combination of stuffover pad construction in the back and arms with a sprung stuffover seat base.

Rip down/strip out to the muslin (calico).

Inside arms (IAs) and inside back (IB) – stuffover pads

Mark out, position, and fix webbing to the frame, staying inside the frame markings.

Fix 12-oz (340-gram) burlap over the webbing.

Mark out and apply knuckle/fist-tight stuffing ties.

Stuff with loose horsehair or coir.

Set on linen scrim.

Secure the center of the pad with bridle ties and temporary tack the edges of the linen scrim.

Regulate the stuffings and add additional stuffing where required.

Tack off the linen scrim.

Mark out guidelines and make the blind stitches.

Mark out and apply top stitches to form the top roll.

Mark out and apply finger-tight stuffing ties for the second stuffing.

Stuff with a second stuffing of horsehair or coir.

Measure the three pieces of muslin (calico) that will make up the back.

Cut out, machine sew, and set on the muslin (calico), using temporary tacks.

When happy with the fit, permanently tack off the muslin (calico).

Apply a layer of skin batting or cotton felt and then polyester batting.

Measure, cut out, sew, and set on the top cover.

Tack down the top edge and the leading edges at the front of the arms, forming pleats where required. Temporary tack the bottom edge.

Seat—sprung stuffover pad

Mark out, position, and fix the webbing to the frame, staying inside the frame markings.

Plan out the spring positions, ensuring even distribution, and secure the springs with spring ties.

Stabilize the springs by lashing them with laid cord.

Fix the 12-oz (340-gram) burlap over the springs and apply a second set of spring ties to attach them to the burlap.

Mark out and apply stuffing ties.

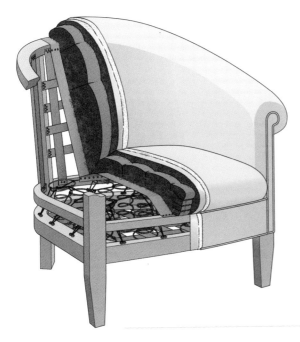

Traditional tub chair

Stuff with loose horsehair or coir.

Set on linen scrim.

Secure the center of the pad with bridle ties, and temporary tack the edges of the linen scrim.

Regulate the stuffings and add additional stuffing where required.

Tack off the linen scrim.

Mark out guidelines and make the blind stitches.

Mark out and apply top stitches to form the top roll.

Mark out and apply finger-tight stuffing ties for the second stuffing.

Stuff with a second stuffing of horsehair or coir.

Measure, cut out, and set on the muslin (calico), using temporary tacks.

Permanently tack the muslin (calico) in place.

Apply a layer of skin batting or cotton felt and then polyester batting.

Measure, cut out, and set on the top cover, ensuring that there are no rucks in the cloth where the seat, arms and back pull through the frame.

Permanently tack off the internal panels.

Front border, piping and facings

Cut and sew the piping.

Measure the border dimensions and mark onto the frame.

Tack the piping in place.

Back tack the border fabric in place.

Stuff the border with the appropriate thickness of batting.

Temporary tack the border in place.

Permanently tack the border in place.

Apply piping to the front of the arm or sides of the inside back, forming the outline of either the arm facings or the sides of the inside back.

Attach a thin layer of batting to the frame within the piping and pin the facing cover in place.

Hand sew the facings in place.

Outside arms (OAs) and outside back (OB)

Line the outside arms and back with burlap or muslin (calico) and then batting.

Measure the three pieces of top cover that will make up the outside back.

Cut out and machine sew the three pieces together, then temporary tack only the bottom edge of the outside back in place.

Pin the top edge of the inside back and the leading edge of the arms to the frame in preparation for hand sewing.

Hand sew the outside panels, removing the pins as you go.

Permanently tack the bottom edges of the outside panels.

Measure, cut, and fix the bottom cloth.

The chair on the right is a modern take on a tub chair.
The cover has been pre-sewn to enable minimal assembly time for the upholsterer.

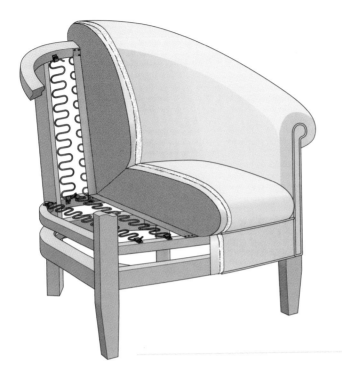

Modern tub chair

A combination of synthetic layered fillings are used in the arms and back construction; I advise using a softer foam in the back than in the seat. The seat will most likely be sprung in some way and may have a combination of foam densities to give a gradual compression when sat in.

Rip down/strip out to the muslin (calico).

Inside arms (IAs) and inside back (IB)

Mark out, position and fix webbing to the frame, staying inside the frame markings.

Fix 12-oz (340-gram) burlap or a synthetic alternative over the webbing.

Mark out, cut, and fix the arm and back foam to the frame.

Measure, cut out, and machine sew the top cover together.

Apply a layer of polyester batting over the foam.

Temporary tack the cover in place.

Tack down the top edge and the leading edges at the front of the arms, forming the arm pleats.

Seat

Mark out and fix either serpentine springs or elasticated webbing to the frame.

If using serpentine springs, lash them with laid cord or a synthetic alternative.

Mark out and cut a piece or pieces of seating-density foam.

Glue or staple the foam directly to the frame or attach muslin (calico) strips to the foam and staple them onto the frame.

Measure, cut out, and fix polyester batting to the foam, using spray adhesive.

Measure, cut out, and set on the top cover.

Tuck the top cover through the sides and the back and tack off.

Front border, piping and facings

Cut and sew the piping.

Measure the border dimensions and mark onto the frame.

Tack the piping in place.

Back tack the border fabric in place.

Stuff the border with the appropriate thickness of batting.

Temporary tack the border in place.

Permanently tack the border in place.

Apply piping to the front of the arm or sides of the inside back, forming the outline of either the arm facings or the sides of the inside back.

Attach a thin layer of batting to the frame within the piping and pin the facing cover in place.

Hand sew the facings in place.

Outside arms (OAs) and outside back (OB)

Line the outside arms and back with burlap or muslin (calico) and then batting.

Measure the three pieces of top cover that will make up the outside back.

Cut out and machine sew the three pieces together, then temporary tack only the bottom edge of the outside back in place.

Pin the top edge of the inside back and the leading edge of the arms to the frame in preparation for hand sewing.

Hand sew the outside panels, removing the pins as you go.

Permanently tack the bottom edges of the outside panels.

Measure, cut, and fix the bottom cloth.

This is a modern tub chair that uses natural filllings.
It marries traditional craft elements with cutting-edge digital fabric printing techniques.

A traditional hand-stuffed arm chair displaying scrolled arms and a full seat.
It has elements of both wing chair and tub chair.

Traditional wing chair

Wing chair

Traditional wing chair

Using all of the pad types, the arms are usually variations of stuffover pads, the wings are simple pinstuffed pads and the seat is a variation of the sprung stuffover pad.

Rip down.

Inside arms (IAs)—stuffover pads

Mark out, position, and fix webbing to the frame, staying inside the frame markings.

Fix 12-oz (340-gram) burlap over the webbing.

Mark out and apply knuckle/fist-tight stuffing ties.

Stuff with loose horsehair or coir.

Set on linen scrim.

Secure the center of the pad with bridle ties and temporary tack the edges of the linen scrim.

Regulate the stuffings and add additional stuffing where required.

Tack off the linen scrim.

Mark out guidelines and make the blind stitches.

Mark out and apply top stitches to form the top roll.

Mark out and apply finger-tight stuffing ties for the second stuffing.

Stuff with a second stuffing of horsehair or coir.

Measure the piece of muslin (calico) that will cover the inside arm pads.

Cut out and set on the muslin (calico), using temporary tacks.

When happy with the fit, permanently tack off.

Apply a layer of skin batting or cotton felt and then polyester batting.

Measure, cut out, and set on the top cover.

Permanently tack off the front and top of the panels, but leave the bottom edge temporary tacked.

Inside wings (IWs)—pinstuffed pads

Mark out, position and fix webbing to the frame, staying inside the frame markings.

Fix 12-oz (340-gram) burlap over the webbing.

Mark out and apply finger-tight stuffing ties.

Stuff with loose horsehair or coir.

Set on linen scrim.

Secure the center of the pad with bridle ties and temporary tack the edges of the linen scrim.

Regulate the stuffings and add additional stuffing where required.

Tack off the linen scrim.

Mark out and apply finger-tight stuffing ties for the second stuffing.

Stuff with a second stuffing of horsehair or coir.

Measure the muslin (calico) that will cover the inside wing pads.

Cut out and set on the muslin (calico), using temporary tacks.

When happy with the fit, permanently tack off.

Apply a layer of skin batting or cotton felt and then polyester batting.

Measure, cut out, and set on the top cover.

When happy with the placement, permanently tack off the top cover.

Inside back (IB) – stuffover pad

Mark out, position and fix webbing to the frame, staying inside the frame markings.

Fix 12-oz (340-gram) burlap over the webbing.

Mark out and apply knuckle/fist-tight stuffing ties.

Stuff with loose horsehair or coir.

Set on linen scrim.

Secure the center of the pad with bridle ties and temporary tack the edges of the linen scrim.

Regulate the stuffings and add additional stuffing where required.

Tack off the linen scrim.

Mark out and apply top stitches to form the top roll at the top of the inside back.

Mark out and apply finger-tight stuffing ties for the second stuffing.

Stuff with a second stuffing of horsehair or coir.

Measure the piece of muslin (calico) that will cover the inside back fillings.

Cut out and set on the muslin (calico) using temporary tacks.

When happy with the fit, permanently tack off.

Apply a layer of skin batting or cotton felt and then polyester batting.

Measure, cut out, and set on the top cover.

When happy with the placement, permanently tack off the top cover.

Seat – stuffover pad

Mark out, position and fix the webbing to the frame, staying inside the frame markings.

Plan out the spring positions, ensuring even distribution, and secure the springs with spring ties.

Stabilize the springs by lashing them with laid cord.

Fix 12-oz (340-gram) burlap over the springs and apply a second set of spring ties to attach them to the burlap.

Mark out and apply stuffing ties.

Stuff with loose horsehair or coir.

Set on linen scrim.

Secure the center of the pad with bridle ties and temporary tack the edges of the linen scrim.

Regulate the stuffings and add additional stuffing where required.

Tack off the linen scrim.

Mark out guidelines and make the blind stitches.

Mark out and apply top stitches to form the top roll.

Mark out and apply finger-tight stuffing ties for the second stuffing.

Stuff with a second stuffing of horsehair or coir.

Measure, cut out, and set on the muslin (calico), using temporary tacks.

Permanently tack the muslin (calico) in place.

Apply a layer of skin batting or cotton felt and then polyester batting.

Measure, cut out, and set on the top cover.

When happy with the placement, permanently tack off the top cover.

Front border, piping and facings

Cut and sew the piping.

Measure the border dimensions and mark onto the frame.

Tack the piping in place.

Back tack the border fabric in place.

Stuff the border with the appropriate thickness of batting.

Temporarily tack the border in place.

Permanently tack the border in place.

Apply piping to the frame, forming the outline of the arm facings.

Attach a thin layer of batting to the frame within the piping and pin the facing cover in place.

Hand sew the facings in place.

Outside wings (OWs)

Apply piping to the edge of the frame, forming the outside edges of the outside panels.

Line with burlap or muslin (calico).

Measure the top cover that will make up the outside wing.

Temporary tack the bottom and back edges of the wings in place.

Pin the top edge and the leading edge of the wings to the frame in preparation for hand sewing.

Hand sew the outside wings to the inside panels.

Permanently tack the bottom and back edges of the wings to the frame.

Outside arms (OAs)

Back tack the top edge of the outside arm fabric in place.

Line with burlap or muslin (calico) and insert a layer of batting.

Temporary tack the bottom and back edges in place.

Pin the front edge of the outside arms to the frame in preparation for hand sewing.

Hand sew the outside arm panels in place.

Permanently tack the bottom and back edges to the frame.

Outside back (OB)

Line with burlap or muslin (calico).

Measure the top cover that will make up the outside back.

Pin the top edge and temporary tack the bottom edge in place.

Pin down the sides.

Hand sew the outside panels into place.

Permanently tack the bottom edge.

Measure, cut, and fit the bottom cloth.

Modern wing chair

Using several foam types, the arms are usually medium- to firm-density foam, the wings are most effective with firm foam, and the seat is typically sprung with springs or elastic webbing and has one or two layers of foam, with the firmest density over the springs and then a softer layer directly under the polyester batting.

Rip down.

Inside arms (IAs)

Mark out, position and fix webbing to the frame, staying inside the frame markings.

Fix either 12-oz (340-gram) burlap or a synthetic alternative over the webbing.

Mark out and fix the arm foam to the frame either directly, or apply muslin (calico) strips to the foam and then tack them down to the frame.

Measure and cut out the top cover.

Apply a layer of polyester batting over the foam.

Temporary tack the cover into place.

Permanently tack off the front and top of the panels, but leave the bottom edge temporary tacked.

Inside wings (IWs)

Mark out, position, and fix webbing to the frame, staying inside the frame markings.

Fix either 12-oz (340-gram) burlap or a synthetic alternative over the webbing.

Mark out and fix the wing foam to the frame either directly, or apply muslin (calico) strips to the foam and then tack them down to the frame.

Measure and cut out the top cover.

Apply a layer of polyester batting over the foam.

Temporary tack the cover into place.

Permanently tack off the cover all around the wing.

Inside back (IB)

Mark out, position, and fix either webbing or super-loop springs to the frame, staying inside the frame markings.

Fix either 12-oz (340-gram) burlap or a synthetic alternative over the webbing or springs.

Mark out and fix the back foam to the frame.

Measure and cut out the top cover.

Apply a layer of polyester batting over the foam.

Temporary tack the cover into place.

Permanently tack off the top and sides of the panel, but leave the bottom edge temporary tacked.

Seat

Mark out and fix either serpentine springs or elasticated webbing to the frame.

If using serpentine springs, lash them with laid cord or a synthetic alternative.

Mark out and cut a piece of seating-density foam.

Fix the seat foam to the frame either directly or apply muslin (calico) strips to the foam and then tack them down to the frame.

Measure, cut out, and fix polyester batting to the foam, using spray adhesive.

Measure, cut out, and set on the top cover.

Tuck the top cover through the sides and the back and tack off.

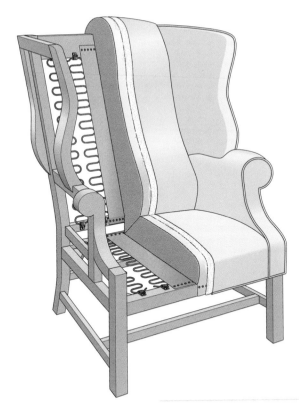

Modern wing chair

Front border, piping, and facings

Cut and sew the piping.

Measure the border dimensions and mark onto the frame.

Tack the piping in place.

Back tack the border fabric in place.

Stuff the border with the appropriate thickness of wadding.

Temporary tack the border in place.

Permanently tack the border in place.

Apply piping to the frame, forming the outline of the arm facings.

Attach a thin layer of wadding to the frame within the piping and pin the cover in place.

Hand sew the facings in place.

Outside wings (OWs)

Apply piping to the edge of the frame forming the outside edges of the outside panels.

Line with burlap or muslin (calico).

Measure the top cover that will make up the outside wing.

Temporary tack the bottom and back edges into place.

Pin the top edge and the leading edge of the wings to the frame in preparation for hand sewing.

Hand sew the outside panels in place.

Permanently tack the bottom and back edges.

Outside arms (OAs)

Back tack the top edge of the outside arm fabric in place.

Line with burlap, muslin (calico) or a synthetic alternative and insert a layer of polyester wadding.

Temporary tack the bottom and back edges in place.

Pin the front edge of the outside arm to the frame in preparation for hand sewing.

Hand sew the outside arm panels in place.

Permanently tack the bottom and back edges.

Outside back (OB)

Line with burlap or muslin (calico).

Measure the top cover that will make up the outside back.

Pin the top edge and temporary tack the bottom edge in place.

Pin down the sides.

Hand sew the outside panels in place.

Permanently tack the bottom edge.

Measure, cut and fit the bottom cloth.

A modern take on a tradtional wing chair .

Glossary

Back tacking: A way of fixing fabric through the reverse face and then folding it back on itself to reveal the top face, so that the fixing is concealed.

Balloon-back chair: Mainly Victorian style of chair with a rounded or oval back, frequently manufactured from mahogany with an upholstered seat (see sprung stuffover dining chair on page 227).

Batting: Either a natural or man-made layer that sits between the filling and cover and adds volume and softness to a pad.

Bias: At a 45-degree angle to the lengthways grain of the fabric. It will stretch significantly more when pulled, as opposed to the warp or weft.

Blind stitch: A stitch that is used to build height into a pad. Evidence of this stitch is only seen on the edge of the pad, hence the term "blind" stitch.

Border: A thinly stuffed pad, usually found at the front of a chair under the lip of the seat.

Bottom or bottoming cloth: A plain, woven cloth, often dyed black, that is attached to the underside of a chair and prevents dust and debris from falling onto the floor as the seat pad degrades.

Braid: Woven strip used as a trimming to mask the point where an upholstered pad meets show wood.

Bridle ties: Stitches used to sandwich stuffing between a layer of 12-oz (340-gram) burlap underneath and linen scrim above.

Canvas: Generic term given to heavyweight fabrics fitted over a suspension system.

Capped on: Shaped pieces of fabric machined together to allow the cover to fit over more complex upholstered shapes without the need for pleats, to enable the shape to form.

Collar: An extra piece of fabric machine sewn around the shape, which allows the main panel of fabric to bend around a separate pad without rucking up or puckering.

Corridor: The area of a pad that is most prominent to the eye. Patterns should align through all corridors on chairs that have multiple corridors.

Crown: The area of the pad that is most prominent physically. Not always in the center of the pad, the crown suggests the overall volume or fullness of the pad.

Dressing the cover: Using your hand to manipulate either fillings or fabric, so that no rucks can be felt under the cover.

Facing: A panel that is typically found at the front of arms or either side of an inside back.

Feather edge: Either a very fine top stitch applied to a stitched edge or a blanket stitch applied to an existing top roll, both of which define a sharper edge to the pad.

Fly: A piece of typically plain and less expensive fabric sewn to the bottom edge of inside backs or arms or the back edge of seats, to save on more expensive top-cover fabric.

Fullness: Excess top-cover material where fabric is manipulated around a pad and forms little puckers or wrinkles; also refers to the volume (thickness) of stuffing in a pad.

Gimp (see braid): Its woven structure lends itself to bending around curves more easily than a straight braid.

Gimp pins: Thin tacks with small heads used to either hold gimp in place or to tack fabric down around legs, where a normal tack would be too obvious. Gimp pins are available in an array of colours.

Lashing: Sometimes referred to as "lacing." Lashes bind springs together to prevent them from separating, and evenly distribute pressure throughout the suspension system.

Laths: Metal straps that form the base of mesh-top spring units.

Lip: Front edge of an upholstered pad.

Lock stitch: A secure back stitch that holds firmly and will not gape open when stretched or tensioned.

Loose pad: A separate upholstered pad that either fits into a frame or is secured to a chair via a removable fixing such as press studs.

Lumbar: Area of the inside back on a chair that correlates with the natural curve in the spine of the sitter. Occasionally referred to as the "swell" of the inside back.

Nap: Nap or pile refers to the direction of brush of the fabric and offers least resistance. The nap should feel smoothest on a seat when it is brushed from back to front.

Notching: Either a single or series of small V-cuts applied to the edge of a fabric panel to denote the point that will be lined up with an additional panel. The Vs should be shallow enough not to be seen once the panels are joined together.

Pinstuffed: A thin upholstered pad that contains no blind or top stitches at the edges.

Piping: Typically, a twisted cord encased by strips of fabric and machine sewn to give them a consistent thickness, used to define the edge of a pad, as a decorative finish.

Pulling point: The points of a piece of fabric where it is best to pull it, so that the minimum number of fixings will be required to allow the fabric to fit the pad.

Re-covering: Applying new fabric over the top of the old pads, without removing existing upholstery.

Regulate: The process of moving loose fillings around and smoothing out inconsistencies in the density of stuffing in a pad, using the regulator tool.

Re-upholstering: Removing the majority of the existing upholstery and re-making the pads from the frame upward prior to covering with either the original or new covers.

Ripping down: Removing the existing upholstery fillings and coverings on an upholstered frame.

Roll edge: A sturdy edge formed in the stuffing through the application of top stitches.

Rucking: Gathers or bunches in the fabric that will either be seen or felt through the surface of the top cover.

Scroll: A curved pad shape, it follows the same method of construction as flatter pads but usually requires pleats in the fabric to bend the cloth around the scroll.

Setting on: All layers of cloth should be set in place with just a few temporary tacks fixed to each edge of the panel, forming a cross of tension in the center of the pad.

Show wood: Typically, polished or painted parts of the frame that will not be covered by upholstery.

Stitched edge: Formed through a combination of blind and top stitches, a stitched edge should retain its shape when the top cover is pulled tightly over it, yet remain slightly flexible.

Stuffing ties: Loops of twine that hold stuffing in place prior to the fitting of the linen scrim.

Stuffover: A stuffover pad sits on top of the frame and has a much thicker layer of stuffing than a drop-in style. The stuffing is secured in place and formed to make an edge that matches the profile of the frame.

Tack ties: Pulls that run along either the warp or the weft of the fabric, probably resulting from the cover being slightly overtight at the point where the pull is formed.

Temporary tack: To knock a tack half into a wooden rail so that it secures any fabric to the frame, but is easy to remove if the fabric needs to be realigned.

Trimming: The generic term given to gimp, braid and fringes.

Warp: The thread that runs along the length of a woven fabric, from front to back or from top to bottom.

Webbing: The generic term given to either natural or synthetic straps that form the foundation of most upholstered pads.

Weft: The thread that runs across the width of a woven fabric, from selvedge to selvedge.

Suppliers

With thanks to the following companies for providing tools and materials

J A Milton Upholstery Supplies Ltd
For all upholstery materials, tools, fabric and braid.
Their School of Excellence also runs courses on upholstery, car trimming and soft furnishing.
Tel: 01691 624023 or visit their online shop at www.jamilton.com

Martins Upholstery Supplies Ltd.
Upholstery supplies for trade customers only.
Unit 25 Alders In. Est., Seven Mile Lane, Mereworth, Maidstone, Kent, ME18 5JG, UK
Tel: 01622 817 575
www.martinsupholstery.co.uk

For more information

The Association of Master Upholsterers & Soft Furnishers (AMUSF)
The Clare Charity Centre, Wycombe Road, Saunderton,
Bucks HP14 4BF, UK
www.upholsterers.co.uk

The Guild of Traditional Upholsterers
27 Cleevelands Avenue, Cheltenham, Gloucestershire, GL50 4PY, UK
www.gtu.org.uk

The Worshipful Company of Upholders
www.upholders.co.uk

About the author

Alex Law has been working as an upholsterer since the late 1980's. He has followed the traditional path from apprentice, through journeyman and on to master upholsterer. Throughout his career Alex has worked in high-end craft workshops as well as developing a deeper understanding of the craft through teaching upholstery at London Metropolitan University alongside day-to-day bench work. He has been awarded recognition for this work from several trade organisations. He now runs the Kent School of Upholstery, based in Faversham, Kent, as well as designing and making collections of upholstery for various clients.

Publishers' thanks

With thanks to Sarah Hoggett for all her hard work throughout the whole process of putting this book together. We couldn't have done it without you!

Photography by Holly Jolliffe
Illustrations by Kang Kuo Chen following original reference from the author.

Thank you to the following individuals for loaning chairs for photography:

p228, dining chairs, Carol Mandeville
p241, armchair, Roy Theobald at Theobald Upholstery
www.theobaldsfurniture.co.uk

And thanks to The London Chair Collective
www.thelondonchaircollective.com

Index